A Student's Guide to

TONI
MORRISON

UNDERSTANDING
LITERATURE

A Student's Guide to

TONI
MORRISON

Lisa A. Crayton

Enslow Publishers, Inc.

40 Industrial Road   PO Box 38
Box 398   Aldershot
Berkeley Heights, NJ 07922   Hants GU12 6BP
USA   UK
http://www.enslow.com

Dedication

To Iris Noble, author, posthumously
Thanks for "Joseph Pulitzer Front Page Pioneer"

and

Dr. Diane Matza, college professor
Thanks for sparking my love of African-American literature

Library of Congress Cataloging-in-Publication Data

Crayton, Lisa A.
    A student's guide to Toni Morrison / Lisa A. Crayton.
       p. cm. — (Understanding literature)
    Includes bibliographical references and index.
    ISBN 0-7660-2436-9
    1. Morrison, Toni—Criticism and interpretation—Juvenile literature.
    2. Women and literature—United States—History—20th century—Juvenile
literature. 3. African Americans in literature—Juvenile literature. I. Title:
Toni Morrison. II. Title. III. Series.
    PS3563.O8749Z613 2006
    813'.54—dc22

                         2005019069

Printed in the United States of America

10 9 8 7 6 5 4 3 2 1

To Our Readers:
We have done our best to make sure all Internet addresses in this book were active
and appropriate when we went to press. However, the author and the publisher have
no control over and assume no liability for the material available on those Internet
sites or on other Web sites they may link to. Any comments or suggestions can be sent
by e-mail to comments@enslow.com or to the address on the back cover.

Every effort has been made to locate all copyright holders of material used in this
book. If any errors or omissions have occurred, corrections will be made in future
editions of this book.

Illustration Credits: AP/Wide World Photos, pp. 19, 27, 122, 127; Bernard
Gotfryd/Woodfin Camp, p. 50; Black River Historical Society, p. 40; Library of
Congress, pp. 100, 104; Moorland-Spingarn Research Center, Howard
University Archives, pp. 43, 45.

Cover Illustration: AP/Wide World Photos (inset); Corel Corporation/
Hemera Technologies, Inc. (background objects).

CONTENTS

HIP-HOP TALES

Toni Morrison's Life and Career

"Foxy G and his ace Kid A were hanging in the park. They romped each day till the sun's last ray and didn't stop till dark."[1]

What sounds like the beginning of a poem or rap song is actually the opening to *Who's Got Game? The Ant or The Grasshopper?,* written by Toni Morrison and her son Slade. Toni Morrison is a famous African-American novelist. She started writing books for children in the 1990s. The *Who's Got Game?* series is based on Aesop's Fables. These stories were written thousands of years ago and feature themes about life. One of Aesop's most familiar fables is "The Tortoise and the Hare."

The *Who's Got Game?* series strives to make these tales useful to today's readers. It adds plot twists, surprise endings, and other literary devices. The authors note, "In our versions the victim might not lose; the timid gets a chance to become strong; the fool can gain insight; the powerful may lose their grip. Anything can happen. *Who's Got Game?* is Aesop live!"[2]

Who's Got Game? The Ant or The Grasshopper? uses hip-hop language and comic-book-style illustrations. It tells the story of how two friends view what is important in life. Foxy G is a hardworking grasshopper. His best friend, Kid A, is a music-loving ant. We learn that during the summer

> They climbed trees, tore up their knees
> Dunked balls and shot hoops from afar
> Swam in the pool where the water was cool
> and sang with their air guitars.[3]

As summer draws to an end Foxy G suggests that it is time to get to work. He wants to make sure they are prepared for the winter. Kid A refuses. Their differing priorities lead to a midwinter confrontation. Who wins the confrontation is left to reader interpretation, but the book clearly underscores the importance of a good work ethic and the need to make wise choices.

Although different from Toni Morrison's usual fiction, the Who's Got Game? series has a common thread. All of her works stretch the imagination.

A MAGICAL WORLD

Imagine a world where the past and present mingle. Legends abound, and all things are seemingly possible. People fly, trees talk, ghosts rise. Welcome to Toni Morrison's magical world of fiction. Ghosts, spirits, mythic characters, and magical events drift through her novels as the present suffuses with memories. Points of view change and blend. Conversations are slow and easy, punctuated with the lyrical vernacular (language) of the old South.[4]

Morrison is one of the world's most respected African-American novelists. She has received the Nobel Prize for Literature, the Pulitzer Prize, and many other awards. Her first book, *The Bluest Eye*, was published in 1970. It did not attract as much attention as Morrison had hoped. She kept writing anyway. Her fame spread.

One reason is because she creates characters that stick in readers' minds. Readers and critics alike praise her complex plots. She writes about a variety of subjects and eras. *Beloved* is set during slavery. *Jazz* is about the Harlem Renaissance. *Paradise* explores the 1970s. Morrison considers the three books as a series. Her works show her interest in historical topics. She says, "I'm interested in the way in which the past affects the present and I think that if we understand a good deal more about history, we automatically

9

HARLEM RENAISSANCE

There was a time when the eyes of the world focused on African- American creativity. Art and literature were especially celebrated. The era was called the Harlem Renaissance.

It was birthed in the 1920s in Harlem, a neighborhood in New York City. During the mass migration of African Americans from the rural, agricultural South to the urban, industrial North (1914–18), many who came to New York settled in Harlem.[5] They wanted jobs. They also wanted freedom from racism. It is estimated that more than 750,000 persons left the South during this time. Of that number, about 175,000 moved to Harlem.[6]

The area soon became a sophisticated literary and artistic center.[7] Writers and artists, many of whom lived in Harlem, began to produce a wide variety of fine and highly original works dealing with African-American life.[8] Soon more magazines, newspapers, and books were being published. Most of these magazines and newspapers did not survive.

Traditional publishers noticed. They wanted to release works by African Americans. Some of the nation's most celebrated writers and poets were first published at this time. These include Claude McKay, Arna Bontemps, James Weldon Johnson, and Langston Hughes. Zora Neale Hurston also began publishing during the Harlem Renaissance. Hurston's book *Their Eyes Were Watching God* became a made-for-TV movie in 2005.

As the literary movement took off, so did a new musical form: jazz. Southern black musicians brought jazz with them to the North and to Harlem.[9] It is still popular today.

The era faded with the Great Depression. The country's troubles made it hard to focus on artistic expression. As it died down, interest in works by African Americans shrank somewhat. Harlem's fame also slipped. That is changing. After leaving office in 2001, former president Bill Clinton rented offices in Harlem, creating new interest in the area. It is a mixed blessing, however. More businesses have moved in, but real estate prices also soared.

understand a great more about contemporary life. Also, there's more of the past for imaginative purposes than there is of the future."[10]

She is not afraid to address complex issues. She does not let us off easy, for each of Toni Morrison's novels contains brutal facts of inhumanity and injustice.[11] Morrison explains, "I'm just trying to look at something without blinking, to see what it is like, or it could have been like, and how that had something to do with the way we live now. Novels are always inquiries for me."[12]

THEMES

Morrison employs six major themes in her works. They are race relations, community and cultural issues, personal identity, relationships, spirituality, and sexuality. She weaves these themes into most of her fiction. She does not sugarcoat them to appeal to readers. Her stories of individualized pain and triumph resonate within the larger African-American experience.[13]

COMMON LITERARY DEVICES

The most common literary devices used by Morrison are irony, symbolism, ambiguity, and call-and-response.

IRONY—*A literary device that usually expresses the opposite, rather than the actual or literal meaning, of a word or phrase.*

Irony is a literary device that conveys the opposite meaning rather than the literal, or actual, meaning of a concept. In *Beloved*, Sweet Home appears to be a special kind of plantation. The plantation's name and original operations appear harmless. Some slaves buy into the image. They believe the plantation is a cozy place to live. They do not realize their mistake until a new "master" arrives. He steps in and reinforces the plantation's role as a place of bondage. Morrison's use of irony is underscored by Paul D. He tells Denver that Sweet Home "wasn't sweet and it sure wasn't home." The meaning of the plantation's name contradicts the condition of slavery. Such contradiction helps the reader better see the problems slaves faced.

Morrison ties irony to symbolism when she uses Sweet Home as the name for the plantation. Symbolism is a literary device that allows a person or thing to represent someone or something else. In Morrison's novels, housing represents more than a place to live. The type and condition of an apartment or house provide a key to a character's income, personality, and relationships.

SYMBOLISM—*A literary device that uses a person or thing to represent someone or something else.*

In *The Bluest Eye*, for example, the Breedloves

live in a run-down apartment. It reflects the family's poverty. Later we learn it also symbolizes how family members view themselves. They feel ugly, so they live in an ugly house.

In Morrison's work flying is a metaphor for several ideas. Perhaps the most important are freedom, abandonment, and control over one's destiny. When Shalimar flies home to Africa in *Song of Solomon*, he is free from all restrictions. He abandons his children and his wife, Ryna. She loses her mind from the grief of a broken heart.

METAPHOR—*A literary device in which one thing is said to be another.*

Ambiguity is another common device of Morrison's. At the end of *Beloved*, the ghost-woman disappears. Morrison does not say why. This is an example of ambiguity in her novel. This device draws readers into a literary work. It allows them to take an event in the story or even the book's outcome and decide for themselves what actually took place.

AMBIGUITY—*The quality of being obscure, in doubt, or uncertain.*

Song of Solomon is another work that ends on an ambiguous note. After Guitar kills Pilate, Milkman turns to him.

> "You want my life?" Milkman was not shouting now. "You need it? Here." Without wiping away the tears, taking a deep breath, or even bending his knees—he leaped. As fleet and bright as a

lodestar he wheeled toward Guitar and it did not matter which one of them would give up his ghost in the killing arms of his brother. For now he knew what Shalimar knew: If you surrendered to the air, you could *ride* it.[14]

Readers wonder about the ending. Did Milkman actually fly off Solomon's Leap? Did he commit suicide? Did he land safely and fight Guitar? Did one of them die? Morrison does not answer any of these questions. Readers must decide.

Morrison's novels also use call-and-response. It invites reader participation. Examples of call-and-response in *Beloved* include Baby Suggs's meetings in the Clearing and the community women's actions that free Sethe from Beloved.

Call-and-response actually originated in Africa as an oral storytelling device. As it developed further during slavery, call-and-response was a means for slaves to communicate with each other. Slaves were not allowed to talk with each other, but they could sing. Call-and-response evolved as a way for slaves to transmit important messages, especially those about upcoming escapes. Only the intended hearers could understand such messages. Hearers would sing their response.

Morrison shows how this worked in *Beloved*. Sweet Home slaves await a signal to escape. When it comes, the signal to run is transmitted in a song. The song means nothing to the slave owners, but it informs slaves of a pending escape.

Today, many African-American churches still use a form of call-and-response, with congregations having opportunities to respond at various times during a religious service.

NARRATIVE STYLE

Versatility is the hallmark of Morrison's narrative style. Each novel is different. She adapts her style to suit the setting of each book.

One constant is Morrison's lyrical style. Her novels, at times, read like poetry or music. Barbara Hill Rigney explains that "Morrison also sings her work . . . Images of music pervade her work, but so also does a musical quality of language, a sound and rhythm that permeate and radiate in every novel."[15] Morrison employs punctuation, dialogue, pacing, and other techniques to achieve lyricism.

The music in her works varies. Her novels include songs. She draws on gospel, Negro spirituals, jazz, the blues, and other types of music. Each of these musical forms has played an important role in African-American history. By including music, she shows its cultural meaning. Music serves as both a method of communication and entertainment for African Americans.

One enjoyable example of her use of music is in *The Bluest Eye*. Poland, one of the three prostitutes who befriend Pecola, sings,

> I know a boy who is sky-soft brown
> I know a boy who is sky-soft brown
> The dirt leaps for joy when his feet touch the ground
> His strut is a peacock
> His eye is burning brass
> His smile is sorghum syrup drippin' slow-sweet to the last
> I know a boy who is sky-soft brown.[16]

The imagery of this delightful song moves the novel along. So does the slave narrative in *Beloved*. It enhances the novel's historical flavor. A narrative offers a first-person account of events. It reads like a journal, or diary, entry.

Morrison switches to a third-person narrator in *The Bluest Eye*. She makes the work more complex by having Claudia share her views both as a child and as an adult. The adult view adds balance. The balance helps readers better understand the flow of events.

The narrative style in *Jazz* is different still. It has an upbeat, musical style that makes the jazz era come alive for readers.

Yes, Morrison's style stretches the imagination. However, it can be daunting. Readers not accustomed to an author style-switching may have difficulty following some of her fiction. It may help to keep an open mind while reading her works.

Language in Living Color

Morrison does not rely on one language pattern. She changes language to create lifelike characters. She employs African-American speech, folklore, and mythology. Characters' language and thoughts reveal their backgrounds, providing clues to every area of their lives.

Holding nothing back, Morrison's characters freely express themselves. Language brings the novel's setting to life, be it a field, back porch, or posh resort. Readers can expect the unexpected—including slang and even profanity—as characters speak from their hearts.

Morrison utilizes language to show a character's change of heart. Milkman hears of Hagar's death after he returns from his ancestral home. He is a changed man, with a better outlook on life. His language and attitude change to reflect this.

Morrison likes to throw in plot twists. Such twists add depth to her fiction. Readers who continue on to the end of each work, despite the complexity of the language and plot, will discover novels worth reading again and again.

CHARACTER TYPES

Barbara Christian notes that:

> [At] first glance, each of her novels may seem to be primarily about one character: Pecola in *The Bluest Eye*, Sula in *Sula*, and Milkman Dead in *Song of Solomon*. But as we read the novels, what impresses us is not only these characters, but their blood relations. The people from whom the major characters derive their sense of themselves are as memorable, as finely drawn, as the focal characters.[17]

Morrison's protagonists are usually characters in transition, journeying through mysterious circumstances and personal histories to the innermost psyche, often to a triumphant discovery of selfhood.[18] People are as varied as the colors in a box of crayons or a painter's palette. They are young and old, rich and poor, sane and insane, good and evil, alive and dead. Morrison never clones her characters. They often struggle with some of the same issues but handle them in a variety of ways. Her body of work contains several contrasting characters.

PROTAGONIST— *The main character of a novel, drama, or other literary work.*

Nobel prize-winning author Toni Morrison

In all her books, the particular concept that is foremost in her mind is divided into different aspects that her characters embody. In *The Bluest Eye*, the idea of physical beauty is looked at in terms of its impact on black girls and women along class lines and skin shade. In *Sula*, the idea of woman is represented by the many female archetypes that the world has invented, from the domineering Eva through the handmaiden Nel to the witch Sula. In *Song of Solomon*, she investigates the meaning of black racial identity, how the common history is responsible for people as diverse as the rebellious Guitar, the materialistic Macon, and the spiritual Pilate. And in *Tar Baby*, where the relationship between class and race is pivotal, Morrison introduces white characters, the wealthy Valerian and his wife, as well as non-American blacks, Gideon and Therese, who are practically serfs in their Caribbean home.[19]

Morrison has a knack for creating complex, memorable characters. Achieving this is not easy. Morrison explains, "The hard part is trying to make characters that aren't easily dismissed—sometimes, even people you admire—in other words, people that are just like us. My job is to make sure that my characters are people just like us. I don't know people that are less complicated than that."[20]

CRITICAL REVIEW

Critics have tried to label Morrison's work. She escapes definition. Her writing does not neatly fit into any specific group. She can also write about multiple issues and eras. She does it well, time and time again. Trudier Harrison contends, "Morrison succeeds in taking her readers into fantastic worlds where fantasy diminishes in direct proportion to our recognition of suffering humanity. She docs not, she maintains, create characters who are larger than life; her conception of life is large enough to contain all of them."[21]

AN AUTHOR'S WORK

Major Themes of Toni Morrison

Morrison returns to six themes in her work. They are race relations, community/cultural issues, personal identity, relationships, spirituality, and sexuality. Denise Heinze points out

> [S]he is a mythbasher in a country where writers have been canonized for creating and perpetuating the myths that form the foundation of the American way of thinking: the cult of domesticity and true womanhood, romantic love and ideal standards of beauty, capitalism and the Protestant work ethic, western culture and its obsession with modern technology, Christianity and science, and the collective notion of reality.[1]

COMMUNITY LIFE

Morrison writes about African Americans and their culture. She probes the heart of the dilemma facing many African Americans struggling to obtain prosperity and independence without severing the ancestral ties that nourish their African-American identities. But most importantly, she tells us a story of the human spirit: its strength, its endurance, and its ability to soar.[2]

RACE RELATIONS

Race relations is a hot topic for Morrison. She focuses on how racism evolved. Morrison shows how it impacts African Americans. All of the major works discussed here—*The Bluest Eye*, *Song of Solomon*, and *Beloved*—revolve around racial issues.

These works also confirm one thing: Morrison's writing is edgy. She writes about topics that many authors avoid. She neither preaches nor pacifies. Readers choose whether to agree or disagree with viewpoints expressed by her main characters. Trudier Harris argues that "[n]ationally, we certainly owe Toni Morrison more than mere groupie applause. She has been in the forefront of stamping diversity upon the face of American literature."[3]

It is not an accident that Morrison is in the forefront. She is a pioneering author who cares about race relations. Morrison tells us that she feels "personally sorrowful about black-and-white relations a lot of the time because black people have always been used as a buffer in this country between powers to prevent class war, to prevent other kinds of real conflagrations [fires or troubles]."[4]

Even though she cares, Morrison finds it hard to write about some issues. She felt that way about the legacy of slavery, which she focuses on in *Beloved*. In an interview she explains her feelings: "I had this terrible reluctance about dwelling on that era," she said. "Then I realized I didn't know anything about it, really, and I was overwhelmed by how long it was. Suddenly the time—300 years—began to drown me."[5]

She did not let the feeling stop her from writing *Beloved*. Many critics contend it is her best work. It reveals the many awful ways slaves were treated. It also looks at how they coped when first freed. Thus, *Beloved* compels readers to remember the trauma and horror of slavery and its lasting legacy in the United States.

She recalls, "I thought this has got to be the least read of all the books I've written because it is about something that the characters don't want to remember, I don't want to remember, black people don't want to remember, white people don't want to remember. I mean it's national amnesia."[6] Every time *Beloved* is read, the veil of amnesia lifts. Her dedication to those who lived as slaves guarantees they will not be forgotten.

Personal Identity

Although the United States's history of racism and slavery is central to Morrison's body of work, her novels transcend these issues to envelop truths about the human condition, the problems we all face.[7]

Personal identity tops the list. Morrison examines this theme by looking at it in two ways. She reveals how people discover who they are. She also shows how characters can lose their sense of who they are. Identity is linked to names. Names offer clues to a character's personality or values. Sometimes a name may not be an appropriate one, but it fits somehow.

In *Song of Solomon*, Milkman learns that his ancestor's real name is not Dead. The name was given to Milkman's ancestor by a drunken soldier. He could not understand the name provided him, so he wrote down what he thought he heard. Over time the name stuck. It is a perfect description for a family that is cold and uncaring.

Nicknames come into play, too. Nicknames are often appropriate in Morrison's novels, denoting truths about character, revealing secrets, determining how a person is viewed by a particular community.[8] That is true in *Song of Solomon*. Milkman does not learn the meaning of his nickname. We learn he was breastfed too long. The town's gossip, witnessing the act, called the boy a milkman. The name relates to Ruth's emotional dependency on her son.

Morrison also delves into spiritual topics, which may pinpoint another meaning of Milkman's name. First Corinthians, the book for which Milkman's sister is named, talks about the need for spiritual growth. The Biblical narrator says:

> And I, brethren, could not speak to you as to spiritual people but as to carnal, as to babes in Christ. I fed you with milk and not with solid food; for until now you were not able to receive it, and even now you are still not able.[9]

The author associates solid food with being mature and milk with childishness. An immature person in this context could rightly be called a milkman. Looked at that way, Milkman's name is appropriate. He is an emotional baby. He relies on his parents for basic needs. He avoids commitment, and even when he becomes a man, he is not willing to take responsibility for his actions.

In Morrison's work there is often a search for identity. Characters struggle with the question, Who am I? Sometimes a quest is successful. Milkman's search changes his life. Other times the search is futile. Pecola Breedlove in *The Bluest Eye* is an example

Toni Morrison speaks before the "Mocha Moms,"
a national support group for at-home parents of
color, in October 2003.

of a character who actually loses her identity. Pecola hates herself. She hates her culture. Like Pecola, other of Morrison's characters never rediscover their identity.

Pecola proves that the way a person views herself matters. Self-perception can hinder or help a search for identity. Morrison shows this by contrasting eyesight and vision. The first is simply the ability to see, a physical function. It is external and really does not have a great impact on a person's mind. The second refers to how people view themselves, others, and the world. Because vision is internal reflection, it is subjective. Pecola Breedlove's main problem was internal. She did not have a satisfactory or proper vision of herself.

Vision affects relationships. People whose vision of themselves is not satisfactory usually have a hard time bonding with others. Paul D in *Beloved* is a good example. He sees himself as having a tin heart. That vision causes him to avoid romantic relationships. Once his vision changes, he actively seeks Sethe's love.

Vision and beauty are linked in *The Bluest Eye*. Pecola believes she is ugly but longs to be pretty.

> It had occurred to Pecola some time ago that if her eyes, those eyes that held the pictures, and knew the sights—if those eyes of hers were different, that is to say, beautiful, she herself would be

different. Her teeth were good, and at least her nose was not big and flat like some of those who were thought so cute. If she looked different, beautiful, maybe Cholly would be different, and Mrs. Breedlove too. Maybe they'd say, "Why, look at pretty-eyed Pecola. We mustn't do bad things in front of those pretty eyes."[10]

RELATIONSHIPS

The relationships in Morrison's works are complex. There is no ideal relationship. Morrison examines why this is the case. She often looks at female friendships and romantic love. Friendships between women are the focal point of *Sula*. Morrison quips, "I wrote *Sula* based on this theoretically brand-new idea: Women should be friends with one another."[11]

Morrison turns up the heat on romantic relationships in some of her novels. In *Song of Solomon*, for example, both Hagar and Ryna lose their minds over the men they love. Susan Byrd tells Milkman, "You don't hear about women like that anymore, but there used to be more—the kind of woman who couldn't live without a particular man. And when the man left, they lost their minds, or died or something."[12] Byrd's words foreshadow Hagar's death. She dies of a broken heart after Milkman ruthlessly rejects her.

Before she dies, Hagar's crazed desire to kill Milkman draws community attention.

> Women watched her out of their windows. Men looked up from their checker games and wondered if she'd make it this time. The lengths to which lost love drove men and woman never surprised them. They had seen women pull their dresses over their heads and howl like dogs for lost love. And men who sat in doorways with pennies in their mouths for lost love. "Thank God," they whispered to themselves, "thank God I ain't never had one of them graveyard loves."[13]

"Graveyard love" is a term for a really bad relationship. It means to love someone so much, you do not care about anything else. It is, therefore, obsessive. When a person's love is not returned, he or she can become bitter or brokenhearted. Ryna is Hagar's ancestor. They both died from broken hearts. Their deaths demonstrate how some relationship problems can occur in multiple generations of one family. Morrison also explores this idea in other works.

SPIRITUALITY AND THE SUPERNATURAL

Beloved ranks high among Morrison's novels with a spiritual or supernatural theme. Beloved is a key character. She seems to be the ghost of a murdered child. Most characters—and readers—believe this is the case, but we cannot be certain. True to her use of ambiguity, Morrison never confirms this assumption.

Beloved first haunts 124 Bluestone, and later appears at the house as a twenty-year-old woman. She moves into 124. Her malicious, vindictive presence is obvious in the opening paragraph of the novel.

> 124 was spiteful. Full of a baby's venom. The women in the house knew it and so did the children. For years each put up with the spite in his own way, but by 1873 Sethe and her daughter Denver were its only victims.[14]

Venom is usually associated with snakes. Morrison introduces Beloved as a poisonous influence with the use of the word. She is a deadly connection to the past, causing more harm than good. Beloved's disappearance frees Sethe, Paul D, Denver, and the community from the guilt of the past. Remaining free of Beloved's consuming supernatural influence takes a conscious effort.

> So they forgot her. Like an unpleasant dream during a troubling sleep. Occasionally, however, the rustle of a skirt hushes when they wake, and the knuckles brushing a cheek in sleep seem to belong to the sleeper. Sometimes the photograph of a close friend or relative—looked at too long—shifts, and something more familiar than the dear

face itself moves there. They can touch it if they like, but don't, because they know things will never be the same if they do.[15]

Besides ghosts and spirits, Morrison's treatment of spirituality or supernatural themes includes Christian and other religious beliefs.

Morrison writes about spirituality and the supernatural, but never portrays them as always beneficial or accepted. *Paradise* is a good example. The story revolves around the fictional town Ruby, Oklahoma. The focus is on a run-down convent. A community of women live there. Conflicts arise due to religious bigotry. Other issues come into play.

The Bluest Eye also examines spiritual themes. Soaphead Church calls himself a reader, adviser, and interpreter of dreams. His name and title appear to indicate a clean, spiritual, and moral life. Readers learn that this is not so. Soaphead Church is a phony. He has no powers.

Moreover, Soaphead shuns women but likes touching young girls' breasts. While Soaphead's actions are inappropriate, he sees them as innocent and tender. Indeed, in the present-day world, Soaphead would be considered a pedophile—an adult who inappropriately engages in some form of sexual contact with a minor.

SEXUALITY

Sexuality is complex. Morrison portrays sexual relations in both a positive and negative light. She addresses incest, rape, adultery, and other sensitive sexual topics. She does so to reveal characters' flaws. In *Song of Solomon*, Milkman's selfishness is evident. He does not respect women. He carelessly dumps them. He is especially cruel to his cousin Hagar. They have a sexual relationship for more than twelve years. One day he dumps her.

In *The Bluest Eye* we learn why Miss Della Jones's husband left her for another woman. She was too clean for him—sexually and spiritually.

> "Well somebody asked him why he left a nice good church woman like Della for that heifer. You know Della always did keep a clean house. And he said the honest-to-God real reason was he couldn't take no more of that violet water Della Jones used. Said he wanted a woman to smell like a woman. Said Della was just too clean for him."[16]

FEMINIST PROSE

Morrison has often been seen as a pioneer among women writers. Emerging in an era when African-American writing was seen as a predominantly male endeavor and women writers were perceived as predominantly white, she redefined the role of "black woman writer."[17] Critic Barbara Christian notes,

> The development of Afro-American women's fiction is, in many instances, a mirror image of the intensity of the relationship between sexism and racism in this country. And while many of us may grasp this fact in terms of economics or social status, we often forget the toll it takes in terms of self-expression and therefore self-empowerment. To be able to use the range of one's voice, to attempt to express the totality of self, is a recurring struggle in the tradition of . . . writers from the nineteenth century to the present.[18]

Since sex and race have been so interrelated in the history of the United States, it is not surprising that when black women published novels, they necessarily reflected on that relationship, whether they intended to or not.[19] But, says Barbara Rigney, "Clearly there are no 'whole truths' or 'whole' men and women in Morrison's novels, at least not in any traditional fictional sense. Just as she challenges the dominant cultural view of language and signification, so Morrison also subverts traditional Western notions of identity and wholeness."[20]

Morrison's works have been studied by numerous critics. Some include Barbara Christian; Houston A. Baker, Jr.; and Henry Louis Gates, Jr. She faced the unrelentingly negative attitudes of many critics toward her work because, and she herself maintains, critics lack understanding of the culture, the world, the given quality out of which she writes.[21] A survey of the books and articles written about Morrison's work clearly indicates that hers is perceived to be among the most elusive in terms of interpreting and categorizing. Many different systematic critical approaches have been tried: existential, feminist, romantic, archetypal, or Marxist, just to name a few.[22]

Many critics consider Morrison primarily a feminist writer. This is because her works often center around women's experiences and are told from their viewpoints. Her work, therefore, does not rely on male-dominated views and traditional viewpoints of women's roles. According to Maria Lauret:

> It was not until the demise of Black militancy in the early 1970s, when African-American feminists began to articulate their critiques of white feminism as well as Black gender relations, that a self-identified Black feminist cultural practice began to emerge in the work of Maya Angelou, Toni Morrison, Toni Cade Bambara, Gloria Naylor, and Alice Walker. . . . [T]his new fiction differed from 1960s counter-cultural writing not only in its positive representation of strong black women, but perhaps particularly in its return to the language and rural setting of the American South and West as a 'feminine' space, in contrast to the

urban ghettos and street culture where their male literary peers found their inspiration.[23]

Morrison says she is not a feminist. When asked whether *Paradise* was a feminist novel, she replied, "Not at all. I would never write any 'ist.' I don't write 'ist' novels."[24] Her reasoning? She notes that

> [i]n order to be as free as I possibly can, in my own imagination, I can't take positions that are closed. Everything I've ever done, in the writing world, has been to expand articulation, rather than to close it, to open doors, sometimes, not even closing the book—leaving the endings open for reinterpretation, revisitation, a little ambiguity. I detest and loathe [those categories]. I think it's off-putting to some readers, who may feel that I'm involved in writing some kind of feminist tract. I don't subscribe to patriarchy, and I don't think it should be substituted with matriarchy. I think it's a question of equitable access, and opening doors to all sorts of things.[25]

CHAPTER 3

THE DANCING MIND

Background of Toni Morrison

Authors are often told to "write what you know." In other words, they are encouraged to write about familiar topics and subjects. Morrison rejects that writing rule. She pens what she knows—and also what she does not know. Morrison explains that "[m]ost of my writing about the black public, the black family, the black community is part of my life, but a lot of it was inquiry. I never lived in a black neighborhood."[1]

LIFE IN LORAIN

Morrison was born on February 18, 1931, in Lorain, Ohio. She was born into a family of four children. Her parents were George and Ramah Wofford. They gave their second child the name Chloe Anthony. The poor couple was originally from the South. Her father moved to the North as a teenager. Her mother's family migrated to the North when she was a child. The cross-country moves were a means of seeking a better life, with more job opportunities and less racial tension.

Lorain was a racially mixed town. African Americans, Europeans, and Mexicans lived near each other. Times were tough for Morrison's family. The United States was still in the grip of the Great Depression. During that era, unemployment was high. Many banks and other institutions closed down. Morrison's father worked as much as he could, but jobs were scarce.

Something else was happening in the country. It was the end of the Harlem Renaissance. The era had opened doors for the future works of writers like Morrison. Years later, she would examine the era in her novel.

FAMILY OF STORYTELLERS

Morrison came from a family who shared oral stories. That foundation helped her to write great stories. She has said she was born into a family of storytellers, and considers her father's folktales, her mother's singing, and her grandmother's number games all as examples of the uniquely African-American language she absorbed as a child.[2]

Storytelling comes alive in her work. For example, Sethe tells stories to Beloved. The tales help Beloved learn more about Sethe.

> It amazed Sethe (as much as it pleased Beloved) because every mention of her past life hurt. Everything in it was painful or lost. She and Baby Suggs had agreed without saying so that it was unspeakable; to Denver's inquiries Sethe gave short replies or rambling incomplete reveries. Even with Paul D, who had shared some of it and to whom she could talk with at least a measure of calm, the hurt was always there—like a tender place in the corner of her mouth that the bit left.[3]

EARLY SCHOOL YEARS

Morrison once hoped to be a dancer. Her dream did not come true. She let the dream die. She did well in school. Morrison recalls being the only first grader in her class who could read. This academic beginning set the stage for Morrison's future success.

She was an honors student at Lorain High School. She enjoyed reading books by Russian, French, and English novelists. Her early favorites included the Russian writers Tolstoy and Dostoyevsky,

Senior class photo of Chloe Wofford (Toni Morrison) from the 1949 Lorain High School Yearbook.

French author Gustave Flaubert, and English novelist Jane Austen.[4]

COLLEGE BOUND

Morrison went on to attend Howard University in Washington, D.C. The predominantly African-American school is one of the original "historic black colleges and universities" established for African Americans. The schools were needed because African-American students were barred from many colleges.

College proved a life-changing experience for Morrison in many ways. It was at Howard that she first became known as Toni. She decided to use the nickname because classmates had difficulty pronouncing her first name. Toni was a nickname for

PSEUDONYM—*A fictitious name by which a writer chooses to be known; a pen name.*

her middle name, Anthony, and much easier to pronounce than Chloe. She would eventually publish her fiction under this pseudonym.

Morrison pursued her love for literature. She studied English and American classics. She was pleased with her classes but dissatisfied with campus living. Unlike her, most students were more interested in socializing than studying. This was unsettling. She expected students to be more like bookworms than party animals. College life soon improved. She joined the Howard University Players. The theater group renewed Morrison's passion for drama. The group performed in on-campus drama productions during the school year. In the summer they toured throughout the South performing various plays.

In 1953 she graduated with a bachelor of arts degree in English. She also completed a minor in the classics. Morrison's school days were not over. She dreamed of becoming a college professor. To do so, she continued her studies. She attended Cornell University in New York. She graduated in 1955 with a master of arts degree in English.

Her first teaching job was in Texas. She taught English at Texas Southern University in Houston. She left there in 1957 for a job teaching English at her alma mater, Howard University.

While working at Howard, Morrison joined a writers' group. It was a turning point in her life. One of the projects she completed in 1962 was a story about a young girl who wanted blue eyes. She later developed that story into *The Bluest Eye*.

FAMILY LIFE

The move from Texas to Washington, D.C., changed her life in another way. She met and married a Jamaican architect named Harold Morrison. The

Chloe Wofford (Toni Morrison) in a Howard University Players production of Shakespeare's *Richard III.*

couple had two sons. Harold Ford Morrison was born in 1961. Slade Kevin Morrison was born three years later.

Morrison continued with the writing group. By this time, writing was not just a joy for Morrison, it was a way to escape her marital problems. Eventually the marriage failed. Morrison and her husband divorced in 1964, when she was pregnant with Slade. She left Howard University, moving back home to Lorain, Ohio. She did not stay long. After her son was born, she took her family to upstate New York. She moved there for a new job, her first editing position with Random House publishers.

Two years later the family was on the move again. This time to New York City. Morrison had accepted a new position at her company's headquarters. The new job as senior editor allowed her to work with many African-American authors. It helped Morrison decide to write a novel. *The Bluest Eye* was published in 1970.

Initially, she did not want to use Toni as a pen name. She submitted the novel under her nickname because it was most familiar to the editor. She forgot to tell him that she wanted Chloe to appear on the manuscript. Once *The Bluest Eye* was published, the name Toni Morrison stuck.

Morrison's fame grew. During the 1970s she

Senior class photo of Chloe Wofford (Toni Morrison) from the 1953 Howard University Yearbook.

published two new books and edited others. *Sula* was published in 1973. *Song of Solomon* was published in 1977. It won the National Book Critics Circle Award for fiction.

The 1980s were a decade of change for Morrison. She published *Tar Baby* in 1981. Then in 1983, she took a leap of faith. After working for Random House for twenty years, she resigned from her editing job, leaving to write full-time. In the years following, she would publish *Beloved* (1987), *Jazz* (1992), *Paradise* (1998), and *Love* (2003).

BACK TO SCHOOL

Morrison found a way to combine her writing and teaching. She taught college classes at the State University of New York at Albany, Yale, and Bard College. In 1989 Morrison accepted a post with Princeton University. She became the first African-American woman to hold a named chair at an Ivy League school.

A named chair is a specific professorship at a university that is named for the person or organization that sponsors and funds it or someone of their choice. It is generally awarded to a prominent professor in the field. Morrison was awarded a professorship named for a past president of Princeton.

HONORS FOR NOVELS

Trudier Harris writes, "By 1990 when Italy awarded Morrison the Chianti Ruffino Antico Fattore literary award, its highest literary honor, there were few scholars, students, or general American readers who were unfamiliar with her work. It was the first time the Italian prize, the equivalent of the American Book Awards, was granted to a black person or to a woman."[5]

Morrison has received many others honors. Her literary awards include the National Book Critics Circle Award (1977 for *Song of Solomon*), the Matrix Award (book category), and the Pulitzer Prize (1988 for *Beloved*). Other major awards include the 1996 National Book Foundation Medal for Distinguished Contribution to American Letters, the Pearl Buck Award (1994), the title of Commander of the Order of Arts and Letters (Paris, 1994), and the 1978 Distinguished Writer Award from the American Academy of Arts and Letters.[6]

Morrison made history again in 1993. She was the first African-American woman to be awarded the Nobel Prize for Literature. Trudier Harris was correct in predicting that the honor would be partly responsible for making Morrison's works more and more popular.

The Nobel Prize in Literature will mean that Morrison's works will be ever more popular and ever more available. It means that an African American writer who may once have been viewed as writing against the grain of American literature will be more centrally incorporated into it, indeed acclaimed in a variety of ways. It means that a woman, writing in English, has been recognized as equal to the best writers worldwide. It means that Morrison will become even more the representative artist/spokesperson for African American writers, as Richard Wright was in the 1940s, James Baldwin after him, Ralph Ellison briefly thereafter, and Alice Walker in the 1980s.[7]

She was awarded the National Humanities Medal in 2000. The president of the United States names the winners. The announcement noted:

The 2000 National Humanities Medalists are distinguished individuals who have made extraordinary contributions to American cultural life and thought . . . Through their powers of creativity and vision, the National Humanities Medalists are helping to preserve, interpret and expand the nation's cultural heritage. Their work represents an invaluable public service.[8]

Penguin Putnam's reading guide comments on her many awards. It notes that "[i]n addition to literary awards, a host of colleges and universities have given honorary degrees to [Morrison]. Among them are Harvard, the University of Pennsylvania, Sarah Lawrence College, Dartmouth, Yale, Georgetown, Columbia University, and Brown University."[9]

WRITING SUCCESS

Morrison was pregnant when her marriage dissolved. As a single mom, she had a demanding schedule. However, Morrison found time to write. Ann Geracimos explains that "[Morrison] started writing fiction on the kitchen table at odd hours when her children were in bed."[10]

Of her schedule, Morrison says,

> I do get up very early, embarrassingly early, before there is light, and I write. . . . before that, I've spent a couple of years, probably eighteen months, just thinking about these people, the circumstances, the whole architecture of the book.[11]

Morrison used her time on the New York City subway to think about and plot her novels. As soon as she could, she would write down her thoughts. Morrison explains that she tries "to write when I'm not teaching, which means Fall and most of the Summer."[12]

Morrison wrote about issues and situations that she was passionate about. She has said that she wrote the type of books that she longed to read. She did not care if the themes were controversial. Initially

Toni Morrison and her sons Ford (left) and Slade (right).

The Bluest Eye was not well received, because of its focus on race relations between African Americans and Caucasians. But that did not stop Morrison from writing about the topic again.

She does not worry about writer's block, a psychological condition that interrupts a writer's ability to work. Morrison believes that when the condition strikes her, it is because she is uncertain about the direction of a work. Instead of forcing herself to write, she waits patiently until she has the solution to the particular problem.

INFLUENCES ON MORRISON

Morrison's family was a powerful influence on her career. Her mother's singing and her grandmother's storytelling were key. Harris notes,

> When all the reading is done, when all the stories are told, what remains is language, Morrison's superior ability to weave tales, her uncanny skill at giving distinctive voices to a variety of characters across class, race, and education levels. Scholars and readers have repeatedly commented on Morrison's storytelling ability, and credit the gift in part to the tradition of oral storytelling that surrounded her growing up in Ohio.[13]

Morrison was also influenced by the works of William Faulkner, which she studied in graduate school. She wrote her master's thesis on the works of Faulkner and Virginia Woolf, another acclaimed novelist. A thesis is like a term paper. It analyzes a specific subject. Graduate students must complete a thesis before receiving their degree. Faulkner wrote novels, short stories, and poems. He received the Nobel Prize for Literature in 1949.

THESIS—*A thorough written analysis of a specific subject that students in graduate school must complete.*

Faulkner wrote about race relations, too. One of Faulkner's primary themes is the abuse of African Americans by the Southern whites. Because Faulkner's novels deal with the decay and anguish of the South following the Civil War, they abound in violent and sordid events. But they are grounded in a profound and compassionate humanism that celebrates the tragedy, energy, and humor of ordinary human life.[14] Morrison follows in Faulkner's footsteps. She addresses similar issues, concerns, and themes.

THE SOUTH

Morrison's novels are set in diverse places. There is, nonetheless, a strong Southern influence in her work. Four factors may apply: First, Morrison's family has Southern roots. Second, the South is prominent in Faulkner's works. Third, thousands of African Americans migrated from the North to the South:

> [I]n the movement north, blacks not only migrated to large cities, as so much of Afro-American literature indicates, but to small towns as well. The effect of such a migration on the characters of the novel is a major thematic consideration in *The Bluest Eye*.[15]

A fourth reason may be the major role that racial issues have played in the South:

> Slavery was known as the "peculiar institution" of the South and was protected by the Constitution of the United States . . . When differences with the

North, especially over the issue of the extension of slavery into the federal territories, ultimately appeared insoluble, the South turned (1860–61) the doctrine of states' rights into secession (or independence), which in turn led inevitably to the Civil War. Most of the major battles and campaigns of the war were fought in the South, and by the end of the war, with slavery abolished and most of the area in ruins, the Old South had died.[16]

Morrison revisits the Old South in *The Bluest Eye*. The book secured her literary career. It endeared Morrison to readers. Trudier Harris contends,

In the worlds she has traveled and in the worlds she has created, Toni Morrison has left her imprint upon our imaginations. She has taught us the futility of thinking only in absolutes, for we cannot facilely [easily] conclude that Cholly Breedlove is a beast for raping his daughter, or that Sethe is morally guilty even as we know that she killed her child. She has taught us to trust ancestry and intuition, as Pilate Dead and Baby Suggs do, to wonder about the boundaries between this and other realms, and indeed to push these boundaries as far as we can. She has taught us to see and to question our preconceptions of negligence, racism, deception, evil, and the supernatural—all with the vividness of biblical images unfolding in the mind of a Baptist preacher.[17]

IN THE EYE OF THE BEHOLDER

Examining *The Bluest Eye*

"My Eyes."

"What about your eyes?"

"I want them blue."[1]

The speaker is Pecola Breedlove. She is a poor, unattractive African-American girl. She thinks blue eyes will make her beautiful and popular. Soaphead Church cannot give Pecola what she wants most. That does not stop her from asking him. She is desperate.

Pecola is eleven years old. For as long as she can remember, no one noticed her. So she prays for blue eyes. She wants the bluest blue eyes available to mankind. Such magnificent blue eyes would solve all of her problems. She would be pretty and happy. Her family would be so different. Her father would stop drinking. Her parents would stop fighting. Her brother would stop running away. She would be loved, not ignored. She would see pretty things, act pretty, and live prettily ever after.

Colorful Images

Why would an African-American girl want blue eyes? That is the crux of *The Bluest Eye*. The novel tackles a difficult subject: racial prejudice and its impact on the victim. It focuses on stereotypes, in particular beauty. Pecola Breedlove struggles to survive in a society that glorifies whiteness. She prays for blue eyes because she associates them with beauty, love, and acceptance.

Valerie Boyd notes that "Morrison's first novel takes place in 1941, when Pecola, an innocent and convenient victim of her community's frustration, anger, ignorance, and shame,

> **STEREOTYPE—** *A standard used to define a thing, idea, image, or opinion, in an oversimplified or prejudicial manner.*

becomes a woman. Raped by her father, she gives birth to a stillborn child and then escapes her sense of ugliness into madness, convinced that she has magically been given blue eyes."[2]

Morrison shares her reasons for developing Pecola's character as she did.

> In trying to dramatize the devastation that even casual racial contempt can cause, I chose a unique situation, not a representative one. The extremity

of Pecola's case stemmed largely from a crippled and crippling family—unlike the average black family and unlike the narrator's. But singular as Pecola's life was, I believed some aspects of woundability were lodged in all young girls. In exploring the social and domestic aggression that could cause a child to literally fall apart, I mounted a series of rejections, some routine, some exceptional, some monstrous, all the while trying to avoid complicity in the demonization process Pecola was subjected to. That is, I did not want to dehumanize the characters who trashed Pecola and contributed to her collapse.[3]

Morrison first captured the idea in a short story. Two factors led her to expand it into a novel. She was "inspired by the larger civil rights struggle and by the efforts of blacks to reclaim what she calls their 'racial beauty.'"[4] She also was

inspired by something that wasn't happening much in 1965: the publication of novels by black women. Such books were few and far between— or out of print, as was the case with the works of Zora Neale Hurston, the most prominent black female writer of the first half of the twentieth century. In an interview in the 1983 collection *Black Women Writers at Work*, Morrison explained that she wrote *The Bluest Eye* and *Sula* . . . because "they were books I had wanted to read. No one had written them yet, so I wrote them."[5]

Morrison says that the idea for the book was sparked by a situation from her childhood. She vividly remembers being disgusted by a schoolmate's desire to have blue eyes. In the afterward to the Plume 1994 edition of *The Bluest Eye*, Morrison recalls:

> We had just started elementary school. She said she wanted blue eyes. I looked around to picture her with them and was violently repelled by what I imagined she would look like if she had her wish. The sorrow in her voice seemed to call for sympathy, and I faked it for her, but, astonished by the desecration she proposed, I "got mad" at her instead.[6]

The story is also about the Breedloves' adjustment to urban living. The family had lived in a rural, Southern community. Expectations were high that the move would be positive. It proved otherwise. They were

> recent arrivals to this town whose connection to another place, the South, had been intense and life sustaining if only because they'd had to forge a tradition of survival against great odds. As new inhabitants, and as black people, they are looked down upon by the more established white community of Lorain, Ohio. The black migrants must therefore learn how to survive in this land that is at present a sterile one for them, even as they try to evolve a tradition that is functional in this place. Until they do, their lives will lack coherence.[7]

Cholly Breedlove finds work in a steel mill, while Pauline, his wife, stays at home. Pauline cannot relate to other African-American women. Regional differences between the South and the North make it difficult for Pauline to do so. Barbara Christian explains that "[s]eparated from the rural South, which allowed her privacy and freedom of imagination, and cut off from the tradition of her maternal ancestors, she falls prey to the destructive ideas of physical beauty and romantic love as measures of self-worth. Her life in urban Lorain, Ohio removes her from her customary avenues for expressing herself and for wrestling some meaning out of life. As a result she lays the blame for her misfortunes on her incapacity as a black woman to be beautiful and therefore unworthy of a good life."[8]

Because she was lonely, Pauline depended more and more on Cholly. He did not like that. Pauline's desire to impress other women made her ask for money from her husband. When he could not provide it, she got a job. Money issues turned their happy marriage violent. "Money became the focus of all their discussions, hers for clothes, his for drink. The sad thing was that Pauline did not really care for clothes and makeup. She merely wanted other women to cast favorable glances her way."[9]

FALLING SELF-ESTEEM

Rejection from other women rocks Pauline's self-esteem. They do not like Pauline's hair, because she does not straighten it. They are also mean to Pauline for other reasons. Their actions cause her to hate her African-American heritage.

Philosopher Cornell West contends that *"The Bluest Eye* . . . reveals the devastating effect of pervasive European ideals of beauty on the self-image of young African-American women. Morrison's exposure of the harmful extent to which these white ideals affect the black self-image is a first step toward rejecting these ideals and overcoming the nihilistic self-loathing they engender in blacks."[10]

Like her mother, Pauline, Pecola does not think well of herself. However, she adores Shirley Temple. Pecola adores the perky, blond-haired, blue-eyed child actress. She loves the Shirley Temple cup that she uses while staying with the MacTeers. It strengthens Pecola's desire for blue eyes.

Ignored by her teachers, despised by other adults, reviled by her classmates, and ultimately raped by her father, Pecola experiences ugliness in all its forms, retreating finally into her mad yearning to be the opposite of herself—that is, a white child like the universally beloved Shirley Temple, with the blondest hair and the bluest eyes.[11]

THEMES

Valerie Boyd notes that in *The Bluest Eye*, "Toni Morrison tells an ugly story beautifully."[12] The three major themes of the novel are racial prejudice, racial superiority, and self-perception.

In the novel, most African Americans see white people as the more attractive race. They feel this way because of the media images they are exposed to. Newspapers, magazines, and movies mainly contain images of whites. They are good-looking, having fair skin tones, blond hair, and blue eyes. Few, if any, African Americans appear.

These images lead the African-American characters to believe that beauty depends on a person's skin color. It is a superficial definition of beauty. By these standards white (or light-skinned) is defined as "beautiful" and black (or dark-skinned), "ugly." The result is that most of the African-American characters hate themselves and other African-American people, especially dark-skinned individuals. Morrison calls this syndrome "racial self-loathing."[13]

Self-loathing comes up during interactions among African Americans. Light-skinned people are preferred. They are considered more attractive. They are also treated better. Whites reinforce this perception. They openly prefer lighter-toned African Americans. Take Maureen Peal. Her white teacher treats her better than other students because she sees Maureen as prettier simply because of her fairer skin. Other children want to be her friend for the same reason.

Claudia MacTeer is immune to self-hate. This is shown in her attitude about Shirley Temple. Her sister, Frieda, and Pecola love the white actress. Claudia neither adores nor prefers her. One day Frieda serves Pecola graham crackers and milk in a black-and-white Shirley Temple cup. Claudia recalls,

> Frieda and she had a loving conversation about how cu-ute Shirley Temple was. I couldn't join them in their adoration because I hated Shirley. Not because she was cute, but because she danced with Bojangles, who was *my* friend, *my* uncle, *my* daddy, and who ought to have been soft-shoeing it and chuckling with me. Instead he was enjoying, sharing, giving a lovely dance thing with one of those little white girls whose socks never slid down under their heels.[14]

Racial superiority is the belief that one race is better than another. When people of one race are constantly told they are not as good as people of another race, they start believing it. They begin to hate their racial features and even their culture. Many times they feel ugly and worthless. Family and romantic relationships suffer.

STRUCTURE

Structurally, *The Bluest Eye* is divided into four sections—Autumn, Winter, Spring, and Summer—named for the four seasons of the year. Each section begins with a paragraph from the Dick-and-Jane readers. The words become more and more disjointed with each section. Finally, words and sentences run together. There is no spacing or punctuation.

The Autumn section provides information about the Breedloves' apartment, home life, and personal and family struggles.

The second section is Winter. In this section Morrison gives us a glimpse of Geraldine and her son. She is a well-educated African-American woman. She turns her back on her race. Her son is an emotional mess. He tortures pets and bullies children. He is particularly abusive to Pecola.

In Morrison's Spring section she shares more information about Pauline and Cholly and the situations that shaped their lives, individually and as a couple. It is in this chapter that Pecola is raped. She also comes to believe that Soaphead Church has provided the magic for her to fulfill her dream of having blue eyes. This is not so. He has no powers. He is more devil than savior. Soaphead shuns women but likes touching young girls' breasts. While Soaphead's actions are inappropriate and wrong, he sees them as innocent and tender. Today, Soaphead would be considered a pedophile—an adult who has inappropriate sexual contact with a minor.

The Bluest Eye closes with Summer. While this season is usually one in which the earth is at its fullest and best, Pecola is at her worse. She, in her imagination, has received her blue eyes. Her imaginary friend confirms her delusion.

NARRATIVE STYLE

The Bluest Eye is told from several points of views. One is that of an omniscient (all-knowing) narrator who shares information about characters and events. Claudia MacTeer provides two points of view: her first-person narrative from the perspective of a child is balanced by her retrospective outlook as an adult.

PLOT DEVELOPMENT

It is the summer of 1941 in Lorain, Ohio. The community is still suffering from the effects of the Great Depression. The MacTeers earn a few extra dollars by renting a room to a boarder. (A boarder is a person who pays to stay in someone else's home.) The MacTeers are poor, but they love one another. They are also willing to help others. They allow Pecola to stay with them for a short time. She arrives after her drunk father tries to burn down the building in which they live.

Pecola becomes friends with Claudia and Frieda MacTeer. Pecola is twelve, Claudia is nine, and Frieda is ten. Pecola enjoys getting to know the sisters. She has no other friends.

Each Breedlove is allegedly ugly. Claudia recalls, "No one could have convinced them that they were not relentlessly and aggressively ugly,"[15] adding, "You looked at them and wondered why they were so ugly; you looked closely and could not find the source. Then you realized it came from conviction, their conviction."[16]

The Breedloves' poor self-image affects their relationships with each other and with the community. It spills over into how and where they live. Morrison explains,

> The Breedloves did not live in a storefront because they were having temporary difficulty adjusting to the cutbacks at the plant. They lived there because they were poor and black, and they stayed there because they believed they were ugly. . . . It was though some mysterious all-knowing master had given each a cloak of ugliness to wear, and they had each accepted it without question. The master had said, "You are ugly people." They had looked about themselves and saw nothing to contradict the statement; saw, in fact, support for it leaning

at them from every billboard, every movie, every glance. "Yes," they had said. "You are right." And they took the ugliness in their hands, threw it as a mantle over them, and went about the world with it.[17]

Pecola and her family do not really fit into the community. They live in an old storefront that was once a furniture store. Pecola's father drinks too much and fights with his wife. Her parents' arguments make Pecola want to fade away. Her brother, Sammy, just runs away. Children and adults shun the Breedloves. Pecola becomes the one most dumped on.

Robert Sargent argues that "Pecola is both the communal and familial scapegoat—she is continually defined by other characters as 'Black and ugly.' She also embodies the insanity of trying to be white in order to be loved—in the end blue eyes are not sufficient; she must have the bluest eyes."[18]

People repeatedly call Pecola "black and ugly." The phrase comes across as a double insult and fuels her yearning for blue eyes. The final straw for the Breedloves begins when Pecola returns from her short stay with the MacTeers. She is developing into a young woman. She has experienced her first menstrual cycle. Her blossoming body is the only thing in Pecola's life that appears to be on track.

Plagued by the taunts of other children and unloved at home, Pecola seeks an escape. Pecola's humiliation peaks when her father rapes her. Her mother learns about the incestuous rape and beats Pecola.

Pecola becomes pregnant. Claudia and Frieda are not able to do anything about the most difficult situation Pecola faces, being pregnant with her father's child, but they wish that her unborn baby will survive. They go through a ritual of planting the seeds of marigolds as a magical act of solidarity with their pregnant friend.[19] Their faith is not sufficient. The seeds do not sprout. The baby dies.

Pecola desperately wants a miracle. She seeks the services of Soaphead Church. Like others, Pecola is unaware that he has no magical power. He is actually a religious con man. She asks him to change her eye color. Although he cannot, he devises a scheme to make her believe he can grant her wish. She believes his magic has worked and that she has blue eyes. Pecola, in essence, goes insane. Pecola also creates an imaginary friend. Only this friend can see Pecola's blue eyes.

Trudier Harris asserts that

[h]er journey from self-rejection to ultimate insanity in *The Bluest Eye* charts the course of the individual who finds herself outside of community norms, basically outside community caring. Although the adolescent Claudia, who alternately narrates the tale, and her sister, Frieda, do care

about Pecola, their efforts, exemplified in the "magic" of sacrificing money earned from selling seeds in a childish attempt to alter Pecola's fate, are insufficient to save her.[20]

CHARACTER DEVELOPMENT

The story is primarily about the Breedloves and the MacTeers. Soaphead Church is an essential secondary character.

Pecola Breedlove

Eleven-year-old Pecola, a symbol of the innocent victims of racial prejudice, yearns to be beautiful and accepted. "Long hours she sat looking in the mirror, trying to discover the secret of the ugliness, the ugliness that made her ignored or despised at school, by teachers and classmates alike."[21]

For Pecola, blue eyes are the epitome of beauty. She not only wants blue eyes, she wants the bluest. In order words, she wants the best blue eyes anyone could have. Pecola believes new eyes would become windows to an ideal world in which she would encounter only pleasant circumstances, experience acceptance rather than

EPITOME—*The best example of a characteristic of something.*

67

rejection, and be considered attractive rather than ugly. Unfortunately, such an ideal life remains outside of Pecola's reach.

Pecola tries to escape the pain of watching her parents fight. She tries unsuccessfully to cope in different ways. Morrison writes, "Though the methods varied, the pain was as consistent as it was deep. She struggled between an overwhelming desire that one would kill the other, and a profound wish that she herself would die."[22] During one such fight Pecola begins to pray.

> "Please God," she whispered into the palm of her hand. "Please make me disappear." She squeezed her eyes shut. Little parts of her body faded away. Now slowly, now with a rush. Slowly again. Her fingers went, one by one; then her arms disappeared all the way to the elbow. Her feet now. Yes, that was good. The legs all at once. It was hardest above the thighs. She had to be real still and pull. Her stomach would not go. But finally, it too went away. Then her chest and neck. The face was hard, too. Almost done, almost. Only her tight, tight eyes were left. They were always left.[23]

Cholly Breedlove

A violent alcoholic, Cholly is a bitter man. Ironically, he believes he is emotionally free. That is not the case. Cholly never overcomes being sexually humiliated by two white men who caught him in his first sexual encounter. Cholly's displaced anger at the African-American girl—rather than the white men—carries over into his adult life and relationships.

At times, Cholly can be very tender, as he is when he first meets his wife, Pauline. He makes her feel beautiful by touching the foot other people try to avoid. Other times, he is very violent, especially when he is drunk. He rapes Pecola when he sees her washing dishes. The only thing on his mind is how Pecola reminds him of Pauline as a young woman.

Pauline Breedlove

Pauline Breedlove believes she is ugly. This is partly because she has a deformed foot. Feelings of isolation surfaced when Pauline moved from the South to Ohio, encountering rejection from other African Americans.

> Northern colored folk was different too. Dicty-like. No better than whites for meanness. They could make you feel just as no-count, 'cept I didn't expect it from them. That was the loneliest time of my life. I 'member looking out at them from windows just waiting for Cholly to come home at three o'clock. I didn't even have a cat to talk to.[24]

Her self-hate makes it impossible for Pauline to really love her husband or children—and vice versa.

Her employer calls her Polly. Her family refers to her as Mrs. Breedlove. The formality reveals their chilly relationships. Barbara Rigney informs us that "the diminutive name is totally appropriate in this case, for Pauline has diminished herself through her obsequious dedication to whiteness just as surely as little Pecola is diminished by her desire for blue eyes."[25]

Despite her coldness, Pauline loves romantic movies. She escapes by viewing them. She discovers another world, rich with emotional and physical contentment. The movies spark a love for white people in Pauline. That love enables her to love and highly esteem her white employers. At the same time, she despises and neglects her family. She takes great care of her employers' home but hardly cares for her own. Tender with her employers' daughter, Pauline treats Pecola harshly.

Claudia MacTeer

Claudia MacTeer is one of two sisters who befriend Pecola. She is feisty, nine years old, and independent. Claudia willingly rejects the idea that beauty can only be defined by white standards. Thus, she is free from the self-loathing that other children and adults struggle with.

Frieda MacTeer

Frieda MacTeer is a year older than her sister, Claudia. She is more courageous. Yet she accepts society's definition of white-only beauty. Frieda is the one who decides to buy marigolds.

Soaphead Church

Soaphead Church is a fair-skinned man, originally from the West Indies. He describes himself as a "reader, adviser, and interpreter of dreams." Desperate people pay him to tell their fortunes and provide miracles. They never guess he is a con artist who has no real spiritual gifts. While women are interested in him, Soaphead is turned off by the touch of other people. He secretly likes young girls. But he never admits that touching them is a form of physical abuse.

Pecola asks Soaphead for the miracle of blue eyes. When she leaves, he pens a letter to God. He writes,

> I did what You did not, could not, would not do: I looked at that ugly little black girl, and I loved her. I played You. And it was a good show!

> I, I caused a miracle. I gave her the eyes. I gave her the blue, blue, two blue eyes. Cobalt blue. A streak of it right out of your own blue heaven. No one else will see her blue eyes. But *she* will. And she

will live happily ever after. I, I have found it meet and right to do so.[26]

Soaphead's words are arrogant and illogical. He does not stop to think that his claim to have given Pecola blue eyes is impossible. Paul Weinstein contends, "In his letter to God, Soaphead Church challenges the religious definition of good and the origin of evil. Soaphead accuses God, the very embodiment (or disembodiment) of goodness. Not only does Soaphead refuse responsibility for his own actions, he succeeds in convincing himself that he is equal and finally superior to God."[27]

In addition to these characters, there are several minor ones who are noteworthy. They include China, Poland, and Marie. The trio of prostitutes live above the Breedlove family. They accept Pecola as she is and are always willing to talk to her. Their tales of love and men intrigue Pecola. These shared tidbits are somewhat exaggerated for her. They contrast dramatically with Pecola's first encounter with sex. To Pecola the three prostitutes are friendly faces among the many hostile ones she sees. She does not clearly understand how other residents view the women. She has no clue that their relationships are not based on love. Thus, she never makes the connection that the women are vilified outsiders. They are not respected. In many ways they are not welcome.

USE OF LITERARY DEVICES

Irony and symbolism are the two key literary devices used in *The Bluest Eye*.

Irony

Morrison's use of irony is reflected in her naming of some characters in *The Bluest Eye*, including the Breedloves. In their shabby home there is no breeding of love. There is no closeness. Instead, the environment, personal struggles and other conditions actually breed the opposite. They breed contempt and self-loathing. They breed violence and bitterness. The family's surname may also serve as an allusion to Pecola's rape. Her father feels tenderness toward her before he attacks her.

Morrison also employs irony by naming each chapter after a season. The lives of the characters and the circumstances in the novel, however, often defy normal seasonal conditions. Pecola's life crumbles during summer, a time in which nature is normally at its fullest.

Symbols

Five significant symbols are the Dick-and-Jane series of books, homes/houses, blue eyes, marigolds, and outdoors.

The Dick-and-Jane series was used years ago to teach children to read. In the series the siblings were members of a happy, loving family. They lived with both parents and an adorable dog in a beautiful house. Morrison opens the book and each chapter with a paragraph from the series.

By beginning the novel this way, Morrison is setting up the house as a symbol. A symbol is something in a story that stands for or suggests another thing. In *The Bluest Eye* the type and condition of a family's home is a symbol of its social or financial status.

The Breedlove home may also reflect the family's character or emotional health. Dick and Jane live in a beautiful house. They have a happy, supportive family. The Breedloves, however, live in a decaying apartment. It is a symbol of their poverty. It may also hint at the declining nature of the family's interpersonal relations. According to Barbara Christian,

> From the ugly storefront of the Breedloves to the standardized house of the Dick and Jane primer, the houses in this novel reflect the worth of the their inhabitants according to the norms of the society and emphasize the destructiveness of the hierarchical order . . . [T]he Breedloves fight and destroy each other in their ugly storefront because they come to believe in their own ugliness, their intrinsic unworthiness.[28]

The Dick-and-Jane series also symbolizes the negative change in characters' lives. Morrison distorts the paragraphs as the novel progresses. By the end of book, the words run together. It becomes impossible to decipher where sentences begin and end. Like the words, Pecola's life becomes squeezed. She is forced into maturity. She is boxed into impossible situations. Her life hardly resembles that of the young girl introduced in chapter one.

Another symbol used throughout the book is whiteness, which is associated with the Western world's standard of perfect beauty.

Blue eyes are an important symbol, representing self-hate and racial contempt. Pecola's desire for blue eyes reflects her poor self-image based solely on physical appearance. Pecola associates blue eyes with the beauty, social acceptance, and love enjoyed by middle-class white families.

Marigolds also play an important role in *The Bluest Eye*. Generally, seeds can represent hope as well as the continuing cycle of life. For Frieda and Claudia MacTeer the marigolds represent their hopes for Pecola's unborn baby. If the marigolds prosper, so will the baby. As children, they blame themselves when the marigolds fail to sprout. They mistakenly believe that their unfruitful efforts contributed to the baby's dying. As adults, they come to understand that this is not true. In retrospect, Claudia notes,

> Quiet as it's kept, there were no marigolds in the fall of 1941. We thought, at the time, that it was because Pecola was having her father's baby that the marigolds did not grow. A little examination and much less melancholy would have proved to us that our seeds were not the only ones that did not sprout; nobody's did. Not even the gardens fronting the lake showed marigolds that year. But so deeply concerned were we with the health and safe delivery of Pecola's baby we could only think of nothing but our own magic: if we planted the seeds, and said the right words over them, they would blossom, and everything would be all right.[29]

Morrison uses the term *outdoors* to symbolize homelessness and community separation. Claudia explains that

> [o]utdoors, we knew, was the real terror of life. The threat of being outdoors surfaced frequently in those days. Every possibility of excess was curtailed with it . . . To be put outdoors by a landlord was one thing—unfortunate, but an aspect of life over which you had no control, since you could not control your income. But to be slack enough to put oneself outdoors, or heartless enough to put one's own outdoors—that was criminal.

> There is a difference between being put *out* and being put out*doors*. If you are put out, you go

somewhere else; if you are put outdoors, there is no place to go. The distinction was subtle but final. Outdoors was the end of something, an irrevocable, physical fact, defining and complementing our metaphysical condition.[30]

REVIEWS

Reviews for *The Bluest Eye* appeared in such publications as *Newsweek* and the *Chicago Tribune*. They were mixed. In his favorable review in *The New York Times*, John Leonard wrote, "Miss Morrison exposes the negative of the Dick-and-Jane-and-Mother-and-Father-and-Dog-and-Cat photograph that appears in our reading primers, and she does it with a prose so precise, so faithful to speech and so charged with pain and wonder that the novel becomes poetry. . . . "[31]

In the afterward to the Plume edition, however, Morrison notes, "With very few exceptions, the initial publication of *The Bluest Eye* was like Pecola's life: dismissed, trivialized, misread. And it has taken twenty-five years to gain her the respectful publication this edition is."[32]

The "respectful publication" Morrison refers to is the Plume edition of the novel, which was an Oprah's Book Club selection. It bore the club's logo, and Morrison appeared on Oprah Winfrey's national television show to discuss the novel.

After the book was showcased on the program, sales spiked. This was not the case with its original release. Actually, initial sales of *The Bluest Eye* were modest. Though not a major commercial success at the time, it is now seen as a landmark in American literature, signaling a shift from the white-dominated literary establishment[33] and thus establishing the author's talent and her authoritative voice on the Afro-American experience: historically, sociologically, culturally, and otherwise.[34]

FREEDOM TO FLY

Examining *Song of Solomon*

Song of Solomon is a story about a man's search for personal identity. The title of the novel comes from a song honoring one of the character's ancestors. It also comes from a book of the Bible bearing the same name, and which primarily deals with love. By naming her work in such a way, Morrison establishes love as her chief theme.

Critics and readers adored *Song of Solomon*. It was Morrison's third book. Published in 1977, it won the National Book Critics Circle Award.

Morrison became viewed as an author worth celebrating. Margo Jefferson praised the book in a *Newsweek* review. She said, "Morrison's earlier novels have received high praise; this one is being trumpeted as her major achievement."[1]

NARRATIVE STYLE

Morrison tells the story from a man's perspective. As a woman writer, Morrison found it difficult to write this way. She succeeded by using the men in her family as models. Morrison had obviously drawn from her personal history; the story of Solomon Willis, her grandfather, is the source of this work.[2]

THEMES

The most important themes of *Song of Solomon* are love and the search for personal identity. The two themes are closely tied. Milkman, one of the chief characters, discovers the connection between love and personal identity. Milkman must learn to love himself and others. Only then will he discover who he is and why his life matters.

STRUCTURE

The novel is divided into two parts. The first part details Milkman's life before his life-altering trip. The second focuses on his trip, which leads to Milkman's discovery of his family's roots and newfound self-esteem.

The book begins and ends with men leaping off of high places: Mr. Smith in part one; Milkman in part two. Morrison brings the book full circle with the related incidents. Readers realize, however, that the two men are very different.

LANGUAGE

Song of Solomon is a mix of many types of language. References are made to Greek mythology, African folklore, and biblical texts.

In *Song of Solomon* the use of language matches each character's background. Guitar's rough language denotes his preference for hanging out in the street. It exemplifies the tough persona he adopted over time.

> While Milkman is associated with flying, Guitar . . . is identified with the earth. A natural hunter, he misses the smells and sounds of the woods he had known in the South. He has the clarity of the earth. But like the earth, which is turned soggy with the blood of racism, he is maimed. He uses his natural capacity as a hunter to try to change the situation in which he and his people are caught, and his involvement with The Seven Days is his way of balancing the generations of blacks killed by whites. But in doing so, he must also snuff out his other natural instincts until he becomes totally absorbed with earthy solutions to the evils that surround him.[3]

PLOT DEVELOPMENT

Song of Solomon begins with the death of Robert Smith. The African-American insurance agent commits suicide by jumping off the roof of the town's whites-only hospital. Wearing blue silk wings, he claims he can fly. His artificial wings carry him downward to a painful death.

His death is ironic, as his job was selling life insurance. Money from insurance policies helps people pay for funeral costs and other expenses incurred when a loved one dies. The insurance provides a sense of security. It is far more durable and stable than Mr. Smith's fake wings.

The day after Mr. Smith's leap, Ruth Dead goes into labor. She is admitted at Mercy Hospital, becoming the first African-American person ever treated there. Her newborn son, named Macon after his father, is the first African American born there. The boy is later nicknamed Milkman.

Like Mr. Smith, Milkman is fascinated with flying.

> Mr. Smith's blue silk wings must have left their mark, because when the little boy discovered, at four, the same thing Mr. Smith had learned earlier—that only birds and airplanes could fly— he lost all interest in himself. To have to live without that single gift saddened him and left his imagination so bereft that he appeared dull even to the women who did not hate his mother.[4]

Milkman's disinterest leads to selfishness. He takes advantage of his family and has few friends. His attitude changes somewhat when he meets

Guitar. Guitar is a few years older than Milkman. Poor and streetwise, Guitar introduces Milkman to a different way of life.

Through Guitar, Milkman finally meets his aunt, Pilate, and cousins, Reba and Hagar. Milkman is hooked. He begins visiting Pilate's household quite often. Eventually, Milkman has sexual relations with Hagar. The relationship lasts for more than twelve years.

With few other prospects, Milkman reluctantly joins his father's business. His job is to collect rent from tenants. It fits him perfectly, enabling Milkman to do whatever he wants. At age thirty-two Milkman becomes dissatisfied with his life and desires a change. Moving out of his parent's home becomes his primary goal.

Unfortunately, Milkman has no personal wealth. He gets his money from his father, who later provides a solution to Milkman's dilemma. Macon tells Milkman that he believes Pilate is hiding gold in her house. If Milkman agrees to steal the gold, he can have one-half of all money received when the gold is exchanged for cash. Milkman agrees to the plan, inviting Guitar to help him. He promises Guitar one-third of the profits.

The adventure begins. The friends succeed in grabbing the bag, but to their surprise they actually find a skeleton. Ultimately, the search for gold spurs Milkman's complete transformation. The gold serves as both a blessing and a curse.

The blessing is that Milkman gets a new outlook on life. He finally learns to bond with other African-American men and even has a tender relationship with a woman. He also revisits his ancestral home so Pilate can bury her father's bones. All of these events are indicative of Milkman's newfound maturity.

The gold becomes a curse as it destroys Milkman's only friendship. Greed makes Guitar want to kill Milkman. He falsely believes his friend will cheat him. His first few attempts to kill Milkman fail. He later tries again but ends up murdering Pilate. As she dies, Milkman finally realizes that his aunt always had the capacity to fly. In other words, she was always emotionally free. Her love sustained her flight. Angry at Guitar and ready to spread his wings, Milkman leaps for Guitar. The novel ends.

At the end of the novel, Milkman is more hero than villain, more caring than selfish. It is unlikely that with a newfound sense of identity and purpose, Milkman would commit suicide. Yet readers cannot be certain. Morrison purposely concludes *Song of Solomon* on an ambiguous note. It is unclear whether or not Milkman leaps to his death. It is left to the reader to decide whether he dies, fights or murders

Guitar, or soars away like his great-grandfather Solomon. What is clear is that Milkman has experienced the joy of flying and the related freedom he has long desired. He is free for the first time in his life.

CHARACTER DEVELOPMENT

Milkman Dead

Milkman is the protagonist. At the novel's beginning, Milkman leads a self-centered, noncommitted life. As the only son of a wealthy landowner, Milkman is born into what should have been the ideal American family. His mother stays at home. His father owns a prosperous real estate business. They own a home. But money cannot buy love. Family members are cold and noncommunicative. Milkman's father is also stingy and mean. He abuses his wife for years, until Milkman retaliates. Because of his family background, Milkman feels alienated and unloved.

These feelings spill over into his relationships. He has a tough time making friends and takes advantage of women. Guitar Bains, who is the antithesis of Milkman, becomes Milkman's best friend. But a search for gold later destroys their friendship.

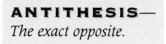

ANTITHESIS—
The exact opposite.

From an early age Milkman is selfish and conceited:

He avoided commitment and strong feelings, and shied away from decisions. He wanted to know as little as possible, to feel only enough to get through the day amiably and to be interesting enough to warrant the curiosity of other people—but not their all-consuming devotion.[5]

Milkman's life-changing quest for gold leads him to his ancestral hometown. One important change is Milkman's new ability to connect with others. Now a man in the fullest sense of the word, Milkman willingly takes responsibility for his actions.

Guitar Bains

Milkman's only friend, Guitar Bains, is a street-smart teen when he first meets Milkman. The name Guitar stuck with him because he longed for one when he was a child but never got it. The name is appropriate because he goes through life longing for the unattainable. Unlike Milkman, Guitar grew up poor. He introduces Milkman to some of his bad habits, including drinking.

Guitar grows from a cocky teenager into a very angry man. He is upset about racist crimes against his people. He eventually joins The Seven Days. This militant group of seven African-American men avenge the deaths of other African Americans. They do so by killing innocent whites. They are copycats. They try to reenact murders that whites committed.

Guitar's preoccupations with avenging murders and with gold alter his life. He loses focus, becoming more committed to the Seven Days and the group's retaliation efforts. Robert Smith's suicide in the beginning of the novel and Guitar's crazed search for gold prove that the Seven Days' tactics may not be as successful as members believe. Trudier Harris notes,

> From using the murder of Emmett Till in Mississippi in 1955 as a backdrop, to the bombing of a church in Birmingham, Alabama, in 1963 that left four little black girls dead, Morrison explores racism and race relations, asserting that the retaliatory violence of the kind that the black vigilante group, the Seven Days, wants to perpetuate against whites is finally unacceptable.[6]

Macon Dead, Jr.

Macon has lots of money, but no friends. Mean and arrogant, Macon is hated by family members, tenants, and others in the community. His wife and children secretly despise him—for good reason:

> Solid, rumbling, likely to erupt without prior notice, Macon kept each member of his family

awkward with fear. His hatred for his wife glittered and sparked in every word he spoke to her. The disappointment he felt in his daughters sifted down on them like ash, dulling their buttery complexions and choking the lilt out of what should have been girlish voices. Under the frozen heat of his glance they tripped over doorsills and dropped the salt cellar into the yolks of their poached eggs. The way he mangled their grace, wit, and self-esteem was the single excitement of their days. Without the tension and drama he ignited, they might not have known what to do with themselves.[7]

Macon is a true American capitalist, as he loves owning property. That fondness dates back to his childhood. Macon witnessed his father's murder by white men intent on stealing the family's land. Afterward, he defines wealth as having land and buildings. He uses his wealth to impress others. It does not work. Townspeople, for example, refer to his expensive car as a hearse, a reference to his last name and personality.

Macon and his sister, Pilate, have not spoken for years due to a mystery surrounding gold they discovered as children. Ironically, the "gold" is really their father's bones, which Pilate keeps in a tarp hanging over her bed. To Pilate, who treasures relationships, the bones are priceless; to Milkman they are worthless.

Ruth Dead

Ruth Dead is the only child of the town's first African-American doctor. Her family gave her the very best education in hopes that she would marry well. Ruth's father agrees to her marriage with Macon. The marriage is a disaster.

Over the years Ruth feels continually lonely and rejected. She comes to the conclusion that her father is the only person who has ever really loved her. Her marriage breaks down due, in part, to an event related to her father's death. Her husband's anger leads to abuse. Morrison writes that Ruth "began her days stunned into stillness by her husband's contempt and ended them wholly animated by it."[8] Ruth's feelings of rejection and loneliness cause her to breastfeed Milkman far longer than necessary. She also copes by frequently visiting her father's grave.

Magdalene and Corinthians Dead

Milkman's sisters, Lena and Corinthians—as they are called—are unmarried. They make red velvet roses by hand, which keeps them occupied when they are children. Their parents expect them to marry one day, but that does not happen. While Corinthians is considered a good catch, she appears too passive and elegant for most men.

She was pretty enough, pleasant enough, and her father had the money they could rely on if needed, but she lacked drive. These men wanted wives who could manage, who were not so well accustomed to middle-class life that they had no ambition, no hunger, no hustle in them. They wanted their wives to like the climbing, the acquiring, and the work it took to maintain status once it was achieved. They wanted wives who would sacrifice themselves and appreciate the hard work and sacrifice of their husbands.[9]

Like Denver in *Beloved*, Corinthians only discovers satisfaction when she moves beyond the comfort of home. For Corinthians, that encompasses employment and a love relationship. The idea of self-sufficiency, especially for women, is a theme found in other Morrison works.

Pilate

Pilate is Macon's unusual sister. The two have not spoken in years for two reasons. First, Macon believes she stole gold. Second, Macon dislikes Pilate's lifestyle, mannerisms, and sloppy appearance.

Pilate and her brother are very different. Macon's life is ruled by money and property. Pilate's life focuses on intangible values—love, respect, family, and loyalty. Macon regards family ties as unimportant;

Pilate fiercely protects her daughter and grand-daughter, who live with her.

In *Song of Solomon*, Pilate represents the stereotypical strong African-American woman. She is independent and daring. Pilate does not live up to society's expectations. Her main source of income comes from illegally brewing and selling alcohol from her run-down shack. To many people, Pilate is simply eccentric, but to Milkman she is a source of inspiration. Pilate is killed by Guitar while on a trip with Milkman to bury her father's bones.

Hagar

Hagar, Pilate's granddaughter and Milkman's cousin, has a long-term relationship with Milkman. Although he is her cousin, this fails to prevent them from becoming involved. She loves Milkman so much that their relationship becomes a measure of her self-worth. Hagar is angry when Milkman breaks up with her after more than twelve years. To get his attention and stay in contact with him, she unsuccessfully tries to murder him. Finally, she dies of a broken heart.

Reba

Reba is Pilate's only child and Hagar's mother. She is known to be very lucky at contests but unlucky in love. The greatest prize she ever wins is a diamond ring in a Sears, Roebuck contest. She actually wins first prize, but because she is African American, the store chooses a second "first place" winner. Reba wears the diamond around her neck until she sells it to pay for Hagar's final shopping spree.

USE OF SPECIFIC LITERARY DEVICES

Morrison employs irony and symbolism in *Song of Solomon*. One example of how Morrison uses irony is in the naming of Mercy Hospital. The town's whites-only medical facility, the hospital refuses to provide health care services to African Americans—hence its nickname, Not Mercy Hospital.

Symbols

Important symbols woven into the novel include flying, red velvet roses, Pilate's navel, money, and names.

In the work a navel represents human life and dependence on others. Pilate's lack of a navel symbolizes her independence from others. She is self-sufficient, as evidenced by her isolated home and her liquor-brewing business. Barbara Christian writes, "Pilate is presented in the novel as the healer of the spirit, the guide to essences beyond outward appearance or material things. But without a navel, she learns how important, though misleading, appearances are to people. Thus, she learns to rely on inner qualities rather than outer manifestations."[10]

Ruth and her daughters make red velvet roses, selling them to various stores. The roses symbolize artificial relationships that may occur in romantic love, family life, and friendships.

Flying is a symbol of freedom, abandonment, and wholeness. Through flying, characters can achieve freedom from something in their past, present, or future. Conversely, characters can also abandon whatever is holding them back and causing them not to fly. In order for Milkman's ancestor Shalimar to fly, he abandons his wife and children. In similar fashion Milkman abandons Hagar as he flies off to search for his ancestral roots. In both cases the women left behind are devastated. Each dies of a broken heart.

Finally, characters can experience emotional wholeness or completeness through flying. *Song of Solomon* begins and ends with an African-American man trying to experience freedom from societal restrictions by actually flying. In the beginning, Robert Smith leaps to his death from the roof of Mercy Hospital, a whites-only facility. At the end of the novel, Milkman jumps off Solomon's Leap, heading toward Guitar, who has just killed Pilate. According to legend, Milkman's great-grandfather had jumped from the same location, flying back to Africa.

The legend surrounding Milkman's relative makes it easy to believe that Pilate has no navel. When Pilate's mother dies during childbirth, the umbilical cord fully detaches without needing to be cut. Upon discovering her secret, many people fear her. Others shun her. Pilate adapts by keeping her stomach hidden. She even hides it from the men she has relationships with. Its absence not only gives Pilate an aura of magic and mystery but also gives Morrison a way of accounting for Pilate's experimental approach to life. From a naturalistic perspective the fact that Pilate has no navel shocks others and has the effect of isolating her from ordinary folk. Therefore, she is forced to see the world from her own point of view. From a symbolic perspective the lack of a navel suggests "that she had not come into this world through normal channels, that she has given birth to herself, in the sense that she has shaped herself as a unique individual."[11]

Money as a symbol of a person's good or bad character magnifies what already exists in that person's heart. Macon is as mean, selfish, and cruel as he is rich. He has plenty of money, but still wants to rob his sister to get gold. For Macon, money represents unquenchable desire. Interestingly, "Song of Solomon" in the Bible is written by one of the wealthiest kings who ever lived. He was also one of the wisest. King Solomon, however, discovered that chasing money and women do not bring happiness.

Meanwhile, the names or nicknames of characters or places also have special meaning in *Song of Solomon*. Harris Trudier notes,

> From a drunken Yankee mistakenly writing down the family surname as "Dead," to "Not Doctor Street," the avenue on which Milkman is born, to Pilate Dead, the aunt who guides Milkman to maturity, to an assortment of other names, nicknames, and pieces of names, Morrison [emphasizes the need] for understanding personal and communal history.[12]

Milkman's first and last name, Pilate, and Mercy Hospital are some of the names that hold great significance in the novel. We discover that Dead is an appropriate name for a family that has difficulty loving themselves and others. "In short," writes Patrick Bryce Bjork, "the atmosphere surrounding the Dead family hardly constitutes what one might call a loving and warm one but is, instead, cold and cruelly comical."[13]

Milkman's grandfather could not read. He chose names for his children by pointing to ones in the

Bible. When he chooses Pilate, the midwife tries to change his mind. She explains that in the Bible, Pilate was one of the persons responsible for the crucifixion of Jesus Christ. Macon Dead thinks it is the perfect name. His wife dies giving birth to Pilate. Since Pilate can also be phonetically pronounced "pil-ot," it is another indirect reference to the theme of flying in the novel. Pilate soars beyond the effects of poverty. Other characters do not have that ability.

First Corinthians's name is also significant. It is taken from the name of a book of the Bible. Chapter thirteen offers insights into unconditional love. By picking this name, Morrison hints at Corinthians's pending love life.

CRITICAL RESPONSE

Reviews were astounding. Among other tributes, the novel was a Book-of-the-Month Club main selection. This was a great honor. Morrison was the first African-American writer to be chosen for this honor since 1940, when Richard Wright's *Native Son* was the main selection.

CHASING GHOSTS

Examining *Beloved*

Beloved is a story about the continuing impact of slavery. Morrison shows this legacy through the lives of former slaves. Morrison dedicated the novel to "Sixty Million and more," which refers to the estimated number of slaves who suffered and died in bondage.

The work shows the link between a person's past, present, and future. Sethe's memories and "rememories" illustrate that the past is almost a tangible part of the present, that there can be no future until the past, no matter how ugly and bloody, has been confronted squarely and placed securely in an appropriately constructive niche.[1]

Beloved is considered Morrison's finest work. Published in 1987, the novel won the Pulitzer Prize for Fiction one year later.

ART IMITATING LIFE

Beloved is based on the true story of Margaret Garner. Garner was a runaway slave. She escaped from Kentucky to Ohio in 1856. She wanted to prevent her children from experiencing the horrors of slavery, but few options existed. When caught, Garner killed her three-year-old daughter. Garner's crime shocked the nation. People could not agree whether Garner was a cruel or loving mother.

The *Cincinnati Enquirer's* original account of the story explains,

> The Abolitionists regard the parents of the murdered child as a hero and heroine, teeming with lofty and holy emotions, who, Virginiuslike would rather imbue their hands in the blood of their offspring than allow them to wear the shackles of slavery, while others look upon them as brutal and unnatural murderers.[2]

The issue was hotly debated. Lawmakers, politicians, and others looked at the case in light of the merits and drawbacks of slavery. One key issue was the definition of *slave*. They had to determine if slaves were people or property. If lawmakers decided that slaves were people, Garner could be found guilty of murder. If they decided slaves were simply property, Garner's conviction would be limited to destruction of property.

Those who favored slavery wanted this latter choice. They knew that if slaves were deemed people, many questions would be raised. One chief question would involve the poor treatment of slaves. In the end, Garner was charged with destroying property and returned to slavery.

Her case had lingering effects. It demonstrated Northern and Southern states's opposing views of slavery. Slavery was a chief cause of the Civil War, an intense four-year battle which began in February 1861 and ended in May 1865.

Abraham Lincoln was president of the United States at this time. During the war he issued the Emancipation Proclamation. This famous document ended slavery. President Lincoln signed it on September 22, 1862. It went into effect January 1, 1863. The war continued on for two more years. The Northern states won. Emancipation prevailed.

Morrison draws from Margaret Garner's experiences to develop Sethe, the novel's main character. Sethe, like Garner, flees from Kentucky to Ohio. She, too, kills a baby daughter, preventing the child's return to slavery.

Morrison explains why she chose to write about the "daily struggle of slaves." She notes,

> I was trying to make it a personal experience. The
> book was not about the institution—Slavery with

This 1815 illustration of a slave caravan captures
some of the suffering endured by slaves as they
are being moved in handcuffs and leg irons.

a capital S. It was about these anonymous people called slaves. What they do to keep on, how they make a life, what they're willing to risk, however long it lasts, in order to relate to one another— that was incredible to me.[3]

THEMES

The legacy of slavery is the chief theme. The novel shows how slaves suffered during and after slavery. Their bodies, souls, and spirits were affected. Enacting legislation did not heal past trauma. Former slaves had to choose to leave their pasts behind.

Sethe and Paul D, for example, must confront past "ghosts" before they are fully free. These ghosts include hurts, fears, and coping mechanisms. Paul D is chief among those who react to circumstances by shutting down their emotions. His determination to only love a little bit falters when he reconnects with Sethe. Although loving Sethe is risky, Paul D meets the challenge.

Sethe, meanwhile, needs to overcome guilt stemming from her daughter Beloved's murder. Getting rid of that guilt opens the door for Sethe to enjoy a loving future with Paul D.

Not all characters rise above their slavery-related experiences. Lady Jones is one who does not. The light-skinned African-American woman suffers from identity issues related to her dual heritage. Morrison tells us that

> Lady Jones was mixed. Gray eyes and yellow wooly hair, every strand of which she hated—though whether it was the color or the texture even she didn't know. She had married the blackest man she could find, had five rainbow-colored children. . . . She believed in her heart that, except for her husband, the whole world (including her children) despised her and her hair.[4]

Slavery's impact extends to the enslaving race. Stamp Paid muses,

> Whitepeople believed that whatever the manners, under each dark skin was a jungle . . . The more colored people spent their strength trying to convince them how gentle they were, how clever and loving, how human, the more they used themselves up to persuade whites of something Negroes believed could not be questioned, the deeper and more tangled the jungle grew inside. But it wasn't the jungle blacks brought with them to this place from the other (livable) place. It was the jungle white folks planted in them. And it grew. It spread. In, through and after life, it spread, until it invaded the whites who had made it. Touched them every one. Changed and altered them. Made them bloody, silly, worse than even they wanted to be, so scared were they of the jungle they had made. The screaming baboon lived

under their own white skin; the red gums were their own.[5]

COMMUNITY UNITY

Slave owners considered African Americans property, not people. They forced African Americans to have children to increase the slave population, but families were usually split up. Children and parents could be sold at any time. As a result, slaves could not maintain the concept of family. African definitions of family were destroyed, and American definitions, denied to the slaves. Thus, understanding of community unity was limited. Emancipation changed that. Free African Americans could choose their spouses, raise their children, and stay connected with extended family members. Such opportunities astonished former slaves like Paul D.

> Once, in Maryland, he met four families of slaves who had all been together for a hundred years: great-grands, grands, mothers, fathers, aunts, uncles, cousins, children. Half white, part white, all black, mixed with Indian. He watched them with awe and envy, and each time he discovered large families of black people he made them identify over and over who each was, what relation, who, in fact, belonged to who.[6]

AM I NOT A MAN AND A BROTHER?

This illustration of a slave pleading for his freedom appeared in British and American antislavery publications in the mid-nineteenth century.

Beloved shows how unity is a key to family and community survival. The Underground Railroad succeeded mainly because people like Stamp Paid and Ella risked their lives to help strangers. Before discouragement steals her spiritual fervor and joy, Baby Suggs serves as a unifying force for the entire community. Likewise, Stamp Paid calls for community unity after learning no one befriended or helped Paul D after he had departed 124 Bluestone. When Stamp Paid mentions to Ella that he does not know where Paul D is, a heated discussion between the two begins.

> "He's sleeping in the church," said Ella.
>
> "The church!" Stamp was shocked and very hurt.
>
> "Yeah. Asked Reverend Pike if he could stay in the clear."
>
> "It's cold as charity in there!"
>
> "I expect he knows that."
>
> "What he do that for?"
>
> "He's a tough proud, seem like."
>
> "He don't have to do that! Any number'll take him in."
>
> Ella turned around to look at Stamp Paid. "Can't nobody read minds long distance. All he have to do is ask somebody."
>
> "Why, Why he have to ask? Can't nobody offer? What's going on? Since when a Blackman come to town have to sleep in a cellar like a dog?"
>
> "Unrile yourself, Stamp."

"Not me. I'm going to stay riled till somebody gets some sense and leastway act like a Christian."[7]

Lack of community unity, fueled by jealousy over Baby Suggs's lavish party, enables the schoolteacher to reach Sethe without her knowledge of the pending threat of recapture. Residents do not sound an alarm, which may have provided ample opportunity for Sethe to escape. Had the community pulled together, events leading to Beloved's death may have turned out differently. But then unity resurfaces. Pulling together, community members provide food for Sethe's household, help Denver get a job, and exorcise Beloved.

LITERARY DEVICES

Symbolism is perhaps the most important literary device used in *Beloved*. Names, songs, and references to the Bible are all major symbols.

Symbolic names include Garner and Sweet Home. Garner is the surname of the owners of Sweet Home, the plantation central to the novel. Garner's name is the same as that of Margaret Garner, the slave whose story inspired Morrison's work. In *Beloved*, Garner is a softhearted slave owner who treats his slaves at Sweet Home plantation better than most slave owners treat them. Sweet Home slaves are neither whipped nor forced to have sexual relations just for the purpose of "breeding" more slaves. Females are assigned less strenuous tasks than males. The males, called Sweet Home men, openly share their thoughts and opinions with Mr. Garner and carry weapons to defend the plantation. Additionally, all Sweet Home slaves are allowed to marry, a situation neither generally accepted nor acknowledged at other plantations. While Sweet Home slaves are treated better than other slaves on neighboring plantations, their names indicate that they are not viewed as individuals worthy of special names. Mr. Garner calls Baby Suggs "Jenny." He dubs Paul D and two other male slaves Paul, while identifying each by a letter of the alphabet. By so doing, Garner denies each man his individual identity. We never discover Beloved's name. She chooses to call herself by the word inscribed on her tombstone. Barbara Hill Rigney contends that

> Sethe's name is one of the few in this novel chosen by a mother, and that name is a mark of blackness and acceptance into tribe and culture. As Nan tells the "small girl Sethe, 'She threw them all away but you. The one from the crew, she threw away on the island. The others from more whites she also threw away. Without names, she threw them. You she gave the name of the "black man"' . . . Whether this name is derived from that

of the Egyptian god Seth, or from the biblical Seth, it represents, like most of the names that Morrison designates as chosen, a sense of heritage and a context of relational identity.[8]

Slaves used songs to communicate secrets, plans, and other things. Peter J. Capuano explains the use of songs in *Beloved*. He writes,

> Often in *Beloved* when characters cannot read or write or even talk about the brutality they experience as slaves, they sing to affirm their participation in life and defend their status as human beings. Song offers slaves the opportunity to express their personal testimonies while remaining within the framework of their larger cultural experiences—all without actually speaking of their shame and trauma.[9]

A Bible verse, Romans 9:25, is inscribed on the page after the dedication for *Beloved*. It reads, "I will call them my people, which were not my people; and her beloved which was not beloved."[10] Used in the context of this novel, that verse could symbolize the end of slavery or Beloved's reincarnation.

REINCARNATION
—*A belief that a person's soul can return after death in another form (human, animal, or otherwise).*

Other major symbols are trees, Paul D's heart, and colors. Trees are symbols of freedom, life, and peace. Paul D and the other Sweet Home men enjoy peace under the trees. Paul D later escapes to freedom by following different varieties of blooming trees. Trees populate the Clearing, where Baby Suggs holds her meetings.

Paul D's "tin tobacco" heart represents sealed emotions. He purposely tries to contain his feelings and experiences. The coping mechanism works until he reunites with Sethe. His relationship with her rips the lid off his emotions, making him recall and feel things he previously wished to forget. Once he opens himself up, however, Paul D is unable to stifle his feelings for Sethe. Thus, he is able to embrace a love-filled future.

Colors have several symbolic meanings. They represent racial differences, hope, and fear. When Baby Suggs retires to bed, she is defeated. She wants only to focus on bright colors, representative of hope, peace, and goodness. She is not willing to focus on black, which to her symbolizes death and bad happenings. Black also represents her oppressed race. Baby Suggs also does not want to see white. To her white represents the men who profited from slavery and oppressed African Americans. Baby Suggs chooses pink over red. In the novel red represents different things at different times. For Baby Suggs red represents blood and bloodshed, a reminder of Sethe's action. *Beloved* associates white with fear and calls white men "men without skin."

PLOT DEVELOPMENT

Sethe flees to Ohio after responding to the call to escape. She heads to her mother-in-law's home. Baby Suggs has already welcomed Sethe's children. Sethe's escape is hindered by the fact that she is nine months pregnant. Bruised and exhausted, she falls down. A young white woman named Amy Denver finds Sethe. Amy encourages Sethe to crawl to a nearby shelter. Once there, Amy takes care of Sethe's aching feet, and later provides help as Sethe delivers a baby girl. The two women separate the next day and never see each other again.

The novel begins eighteen years after Sethe arrives in Ohio. She and her daughter Denver reside alone in Baby Suggs's home at 124 Bluestone Road. Baby Suggs died eight years earlier. Years before, Sethe's sons, spooked by the house being haunted, had run away. Sethe's and Denver's decision to remain in the haunted house results in their isolation from the community. Residents also shun the family because they are outraged that Sethe killed her baby daughter.

That isolation is shattered upon the arrival of Paul D, a former Sweet Home slave and Sethe's friend. Paul D has not seen Sethe in eighteen years. As their relationship develops, so does the strife within the home.

Denver is unhappy about this new relationship for two reasons. First, Beloved is her only friend, and Paul D has chased her from the house. Second, Paul D monopolizes her mother's affection, which Denver wants but is afraid to seek. Ever since Sethe murdered Beloved, Denver has been afraid of her mother.

Shortly after Beloved is banned from the house, she reappears in the form of a woman. Sethe invites her into the home. That decision opens the door for Beloved to begin a different type of haunting.

> Sethe was flattered by Beloved's open, quiet devotion. The same adoration from her daughter (had it been forthcoming) would have annoyed her; made her chill at the thought of having raised a ridiculously dependent child. But the company of this sweet, if peculiar, guest pleased her the way a zealot pleases his teacher.[11]

Paul D is less enamored with Beloved.

> He wanted her out, but Sethe had let her in and he couldn't put her out of a house that wasn't his. It was one thing to beat up a ghost, quite another to throw a helpless coloredgirl out in territory infected by the Klan.[12]

Beloved's obsessive behavior and the truth concerning her death cause Paul D to leave 124 Bluestone. His departure opens the door for a more intense, yet harmful, relationship between Sethe and

111

Beloved. Once Sethe realizes that Beloved is her long-dead daughter, she is elated. That elation does not last as the two women develop a weird dependency upon each other.

Watching the situation evolve, Denver determines to help. She steps out of her home and into the community for the first time in more than a decade.

Once the women in the community hear that Beloved has returned from the dead and is taunting Sethe, they take action. Ultimately, thirty women are responsible for exorcising Beloved from 124 Bluestone and the community. Beloved disappears. She does not return.

Sethe is overcome by the events. Despite Beloved's poisonous nature, Sethe considered Beloved "my best thing." Grief-stricken, Sethe moves into Baby Suggs's bed. She prepares to die in a similar fashion. Her plan is thwarted by Paul D. "Sethe," he says, "me and you, we got more yesterday than anybody. We need some kind of tomorrow."[13]

CHARACTER DEVELOPMENT

Morrison illustrates the legacy of slavery through the lives of six essential characters: Sethe, Denver, Beloved, Paul D, Baby Suggs, and Stamp Paid.

Sethe

Pretty, young Sethe arrives at Sweet Home at age thirteen. Her beauty and availability cause the Sweet Home men to fantasize about her. Yet they do not force themselves upon Sethe but await her selection. Halle's devotion to his mother, as demonstrated by his working extra days to buy her freedom, impresses Sethe. After a year Sethe finally selects Halle. They marry and have three children—two boys, Howard and Buglar, and a daughter, whose actual name is never mentioned.

Despite being allowed to purchase his mother's freedom, Halle never buys into the idea that Mr. Garner is a benevolent slave owner who truly cares about the Sweet Home slaves. Halle's offer to work additional hours to earn money for his mother's freedom backfires when schoolteacher takes over the plantation. No longer allowed to work outside of Sweet Home and restricted in other ways, Halle resigns himself to never being able to pay for his and his family's freedom. Agreeing to an escape plan plotted with the other Sweet Home men, Halle fails to run away in time. Instead, he goes insane after witnessing schoolteacher's nephews physically assault Sethe, stealing her breast milk.

Sethe is pregnant with their fourth child when she escapes to Cincinnati, Ohio, to live with her mother-in-law. Howard and Buglar, sent ahead, are awaiting Sethe, who arrives safely at Baby Suggs's home. For twenty-eight glorious days Sethe enjoys freedom and the luxury of loving her children and living in a community of free African Americans.

That joy is short-circuited when schoolteacher discovers her whereabouts. He and three other gun-toting white men arrive at Baby Suggs's intent on bringing Sethe and her children back to slavery. Sethe, however, is as adamant that her children never experience the life she did. The only way to prevent that, she believes, is to kill herself and her children. She succeeds in killing the child who becomes known after death as Beloved. Sethe spends a short time in prison, and later lives the rest of her life at Baby Suggs's. Her life is plagued by memories of slavery.

She cannot completely forget the atrocities she experienced or feel secure enough to love someone else. In order for Sethe to remain free from Beloved, who first haunts the house, then returns from the dead as a young woman, Sethe must relinquish past hurts and regrets.

Paul D

Paul D, one of the Sweet Home men, finds life as a slave endurable until the plantation comes under the control of a new "master." Emotionally crushed by the abuse he suffers and other slavery-related incidents, Paul D survives with a "tin tobacco" heart, his term for badly bruised emotions. Ultimately, Paul D escapes from Kentucky. He moves from place to place until finding Sethe in Cincinnati. Paul D never expected to begin a romantic relationship with her or to move in. But he does both.

Initially, he stays only a few months. One of the reasons is the guilt and shame he feels for entering into a sexual relationship with Beloved. Another is that Paul D finally discovers that Sethe hurt her children. He is shocked and disgusted, noting, "What you did was wrong, Sethe."[14] He cannot understand how a mother's protective instinct could make her harm her children. In his mind only an animal would do so. "'You got two feet, not four,' he said, and right then a forest sprang up between them; trackless and quiet."[15]

Eventually Paul D returns to Sethe. Beloved has disappeared, Denver is more welcoming, but Sethe appears ready to die. Upon seeing her, Paul D commits to love and take care of her. Paul D's reaction reveals his character development. Wilfred D. Samuel and Clenora Hudson-Weems write,

[Paul's D's] sense of fulfillment comes from within, as his advice to Sethe clearly implies; for he, too, must have reached the realization that he is his own best thing before he could attempt to pass it on. Paul D is finally able to look at Sethe on more than a superficial level. Seeing her for the first time with a more authentic perspective, he comes to accept her as a friend of his mind.[16]

Denver

Denver, the youngest of Sethe's children, is the only child who gets to live with Sethe from infancy through adulthood. An immature young woman, Denver fears venturing outside of her home, mainly because she has been isolated for years from other people.

Ironically, Beloved's arrival makes it possible for Denver to experience life. For most of her life, Denver is a lonely, dependent person who it appears will never have a hope of a normal life. She learns self-sufficiency after seeking help from the community. She thought, "Somebody had to be saved, but unless Denver got work, there would be no one to save, no one to come home to, and no Denver either." For Denver "[i]t was a new thought, having a self to look out for and preserve."[17]

At the end of the novel, it is clear that Denver has experienced a complete emotional and mental transformation.

Beloved

By all evidence, Beloved is Sethe's oldest daughter. Her character is an example of Morrison's ambiguity because we never truly learn who Beloved is. Sethe considers murdering her infant daughter the ultimate act of love and sacrifice. To Beloved it is an act of rejection. Thus, the spiteful ghost of Beloved haunts 124 Bluestone Road until Paul D throws her spirit out of the home.

Beloved reappears as a woman. At least it seems as if the stranger is Sethe's daughter. Her identity is ambiguous; Morrison never clearly tells us who she is.

Beloved is childlike. At first, she seems sweet and loving. After a while, she demands Sethe's complete love, affection, and acceptance. Beloved becomes increasingly obsessed with Sethe and Sethe's past. Possessive and vindictive, she tries to isolate Sethe from everyone else. Beloved's hold on Sethe is broken when community women visit 124 Bluestone. Seeking God's help, they pray and sing. It is not clear what causes Beloved to disappear. Possible causes include the women's actions and Sethe's anger. Whatever the reason, Beloved is gone. Focusing on the present breaks any future hold Beloved may have.

Baby Suggs

Baby Suggs is a free African-American woman. She was freed during slavery. Her son, Halle, bought her freedom by working extra hours. Once free, she relocates to Cincinnati. Two abolitionists help Baby Suggs get a job and provide a house for her to live in. Her home quickly becomes a central meeting place.

> Before 124 and everybody in it had closed down, veiled over and shut away; before it had become the plaything of spirits and the home of the chafed, 124 had been a cheerful, buzzing house where Baby Suggs, holy, loved, cautioned, fed, chastised and soothed. Where not one but two pots simmered on the stove; where the lamp burned all night long. Strangers rested there while children tried on their shoes. Messages were left there, for whoever needed them was sure to stop in one day soon.[18]

Baby Suggs also becomes a spiritual leader to her community. She helps them stay unified.

> Accepting no title of honor before her name, but allowing a small caress after it, she became an unchurched preacher, one who visited pulpits and opened her great heart to those who could use it. . . . When warm weather came, Baby Suggs, holy, followed by every black man, woman and child who could make it through, took her great heart to the Clearing—a wide-open place cut deep in the

woods nobody knew for what at the end of a path known only to deer and whoever cleared the land in the first place. In the heat of every Saturday afternoon, she sat in the clearing while the people awaited among the trees.[19]

Baby Suggs offers fun and laughter. She allows time for men, women, and children to renew their spirits and souls. She changes after Beloved's death. "Her faith, her love, her imagination and her great big old heart began to collapse twenty-eight days after her daughter-in-law arrived."[20]

Upset by the killing, the community shuns Baby Suggs and her family. Over time, only Stamp Paid continues to befriend them. Baby Suggs is heartbroken, refusing to get out of her bed. She stops leading the meeting at the Clearing. She spends time focusing on colors, which symbolizes her desire for nonthreatening activities. She prefers blue, yellow, and pink. Baby Suggs ignores white, which represents white people and their deeds.

Stamp Paid

Ferrying slaves to freedom is a joy for Stamp Paid, a conductor for the Underground Railroad. He changes his name from Joshua to Stamp Paid to reflect the fact that he believes any debt he owed to society is fully paid. Stamp Paid feels he paid the ultimate price when he "handed over his wife to his master's son."[21] Barbara Rigney says that Stamp Paid' s name "represents a rejection of a tradition of white naming as well as a celebration of freedom."[22]

Although his wife returns, Stamp Paid escapes to freedom, later becoming a critical link in the Underground Railroad system. The Underground Railroad was a secretive network of white abolitionists, free African Americans, and former slaves who helped slaves escape from slavery. Members of the network risked their lives providing food, shelter, and other aid to slaves escaping from Southern states to free Northern states.

Because of his activities, Stamp is one of the town's saviors. Well-liked and influential, Stamp is the only community member concerned about events at 124 Bluestone Road.

Ella

Ella cannot forget the devastating sexual assault she experiences at the hands of a white father and son, "whom she called 'the lowest yet.' It was the 'lowest yet' who gave her a disgust for sex and against whom she measured all atrocities."[23] From that point onward, Ella has an aversion to all love, not just romantic relationships. Nobody loved her and she would not have liked it if they had, for she considered love a serious disability.[24] Ella's inability to love others illustrates how a person's past negatively affects all future relationships.

Ella is involved in the Underground Railroad. She assists when Sethe originally comes to town. But Sethe's murder of Beloved ultimately causes Ella to distance herself from the family. She understood Sethe's rage in the shed twenty years ago, but not the way she reacted to it, which Ella thought was prideful and misdirected.[25]

Despite her feelings, Ella steps in to help rid 124 Bluestone of Beloved. She organizes a band of women rescuers because

> [w]hatever Sethe had done, Ella didn't like the idea of past errors taking possession of the present. Sethe's crime was staggering and her pride outstripped even that; but she could not countenance the possibility of sin moving on in the house, unleashed and sassy. Daily life took as much as she had. The future was sunset; the past something to leave behind. And if it didn't stay behind, well, you might have to stomp it out.[26]

Schoolteacher

Schoolteacher takes over Sweet Home plantation after Mr. Garner dies. The coldhearted, cruel overseer transforms Sweet Home into a place of despair and

121

Toni Morrison poses with a copy of her book *Beloved* at a New York City bookstore in September 1987.

fear, from which the slaves flee. He systematically begins a series of reforms that radically alter slaves' lives. Unlike Mr. Garner, schoolteacher rules by force, viciously implementing rules and regulations that shatter the slaves' bodies, minds, and spirits. He adopts a demeaning scientific approach to handling the slaves, treating them like property and viewing them as animals. Morrison uses irony in naming the plantation, which is a place of bondage.

Mr. and Mrs. Garner

Mr. and Mrs. Garner own Sweet Home plantation. They believe they are morally better than their peers because Sweet Home slaves are treated with kindness and respect. Ultimately, however, their actions prove detrimental, as Sweet Home slaves are unable to handle the realities of slavery that exist outside of the Garners' plantation—and thus protection. Morrison's use of irony is further seen in the development of the Garners. The couple treats the slaves as if they are special, but at the same time makes it difficult for them to adjust to the real rigors of slavery.

RANTS AND RAVES

Reviews were positive. Walter Clemons wrote, "At the heart of this astounding book, prose narrative dissolves into a hypnotic, poetic conversation among Sethe, Denver, and the otherworldly Beloved."[27] Other reviewers criticized the reincarnation theme. Yet Morrison thought it was appropriate given the era she wrote about.

Beloved's fame soared. The movie debuted in 1998. *Beloved* starred a cast of famous African-American actors. Talk show host Oprah Winfrey played Sethe. Some critics, such as Scott Galupo, felt the movie was horrible. In a *Washington Times* article he called it a "dismal film."[28] A writer for *Variety* called it a "neutron bomb," suggesting that though it did not destroy the studio that produced it, it effectively killed the careers of many of those involved.[29] Despite such negative criticism of the film adaptation, Morrison's status grew.

SOARING HIGHER

Toni Morrison Today

The 1998 release of *Beloved* the movie was a high point in Morrison's career. Most authors never see their work on film. The movie sparked increased interest in *Beloved*, specifically, and other works by Morrison, generally.

OPRAH CONNECTION

It was not surprising that Oprah Winfrey appeared in *Beloved*. Winfrey often talks about how much she loves Morrison's fiction. She has also named several of Morrison's books as Oprah's Book Club selections. The book club is a special feature of her show. Each time Winfrey chooses a book, she encourages viewers to buy it. Authors, such as Morrison, later appear on the show. Sometimes they discuss their works. Other times they have an opportunity to read from one of their works.

Book sales spike whenever Winfrey announces her Oprah's Book Club choice. John Young argues,

> Before her first Oprah appearance in December, 1996, Morrison was a Nobel and Pulitzer Prize winner, an endowed professor at Princeton University, and one of the most respected voices in contemporary American literature. . . . [S]ince aligning herself with Winfrey, Morrison has become the best-selling author of *Song of Solomon*, nineteen years after its first publication; of *Paradise* . . . probably the least accessible book she has yet written; and of *The Bluest Eye*.[1]

A NEW POST

One year after winning the Pulitzer, Morrison got a key appointment. She was named the Robert F. Goheen Professor in the Humanities. It is perhaps her most important teaching post to date.

NEW PROJECTS

Morrison's more recent works include *Jazz* (1992), *Paradise* (1998), and *Love* (2003). She also has recorded her books on tape. In addition to her novels, she penned *Dreaming Emmett*, a play based on the

Toni Morrison accepts her Nobel prize from King Carl XVI Gustaf of Sweden at the Concert Hall in Stockholm on December 10, 1993.

murder of Emmett Till. The play debuted in Albany, New York, in 1986. One other new project involves children's books. These books did not draw immediate interest. Some publishers doubted if she would make a good children's book author. They also wondered if readers would accept Morrison's entry into a new genre. Morrison kept trying.

Her diligence was rewarded when a publisher gave her a contract. The first book, coauthored with her son Slade, was released in 1999.[2] It is a rhyming picture book entitled *The Big Box*. The second, *The Book of Mean People*, also a picture book, was published in 2002. Morrison next developed with Slade the *Who's Got Game?* series. Books in the series include the 2003 releases *The Ant or The Grasshopper?* and *The Lion or The Mouse? Poppy or The Snake?* came out in 2004.

GENRE—*A class of literary works that usually share a common content or style.*

Morrison's first historical children's book, *Remember: The Journey to School Integration*, was published in 2004. It recalls the road to school integration in the United States. It includes photographs and fictional dialogue of children who lived during the times when schools were being integrated. The book garnered Morrison the 2005 Coretta Scott King Award. That award, presented by the American Library Association, honors "African American authors and illustrators of outstanding books for children and young adults."

In addition to these projects, Morrison penned *Margaret Garner*, an opera based on the slave whose story inspired *Beloved*. The opera's world debut was held at the Detroit Opera House in early 2005.

IMPACT ON AFRICAN-AMERICAN LITERATURE

Two factors are key to Morrison's lasting impact on African-American literature: her job as an editor and the popularity of her own books.

Morrison helped many aspiring writers when she was an editor. Dinita Smith, writing in *The New York Times*, notes that "[at] Random House [Morrison] nurtured black authors who became staples of African-American literature—Angela Davis, June Jordan, Wesley Brown, and Toni Cade Bambara. She also edited *The Black Book*, an anthology of black history."[3]

Morrison's own writing fed readers' appetites for works by black authors. Trudier Harris notes, "In the best of worlds, Morrison's success could open doors for young writers following after her, something that she had indicated in interviews is important to her."[4]

DREAMING EMMETT

Morrison based *Dreaming Emmett* on the true story of Emmett Till. The African-American teenager from Chicago was killed in August 1955 while visiting relatives in Money, Mississippi. He was fourteen years old when he died. Many people credit his death with sparking the civil rights movement in the United States.

Before leaving a local store, Till allegedly whistled at a white woman. That act was considered disrespectful and insulting. Later that evening a group of white men visited his uncle's home. They demanded that Till come out. They tortured and killed him. He was first beaten and then shot. The crime drew national attention after his mother demanded his body be flown back home, then allowed it to be viewed at the funeral.

Approximately 50,000 people, nearly all of them black, turned out for Till's funeral, in an enormous public display of grief and solidarity. Mamie Till ordered the funeral director to place her son in an open casket, and permitted a shocking photograph of Till's corpse to be published in *Jet* magazine and seen across the country. This ignited protests, civil disobedience and a backlash that would consume the South through the '60s.[5]

Two men, relatives of the woman Till supposedly insulted, were tried for kidnapping and murder. They were acquitted. One of the men later admitted to a reporter that he had participated in the murder. Despite this, over the years there have been unsuccessful attempts to solve Till's murder.

At the time Morrison penned *Dreaming Emmett*, which opened in 1986, Till's murder was still unsolved.

In the play, Till comes back from the grave to torment the men and women responsible for his death. By the end of the play, however, the audience learns that the boy is not Emmett Till at all, but another boy who was shot in the back by a white Chicago storekeeper for stealing a kite. "Everyone knows Emmett," he explains, while he is anonymous. He assumed Till's identity so someone would remember he existed.[6]

Six years after Morrison's play debuted, Emmett Till's murder was reinvestigated. On May 11, 2004, the U. S. Justice Department announced it was reopening the case. According to a *60 Minutes* report, the new investigation was "based on evidence suggesting that more than a dozen people may have been involved in the murder of Till, and that at least five of them were still alive."[7]

ENDURING LEGACY

Every year, new readers, including high school and college students, discover her work. Moreover, thanks to technological advances such as audio-books, Morrison's works are more accessible than ever. *Beloved*, for example, can be rented at video stores or purchased on the Internet.

Technology is but one means by which Morrison's legacy is growing. Global efforts also play a role. Her hometown library opened a reading room in her honor. The Toni Morrison Society, started in 1998, hosts events and activities. The society also sponsors workshops for high school teachers who want to teach Morrison's works.

In a world where readers are hungry for fiction that is not formulaic, the answer to who's got game is apparent:

> As a result of her literary and artistic abilities and competence, Toni Morrison stands in the van-guard of contemporary writers of fiction. We must note, however, that her success as a writer tran-scends both her racial identity and gender. She is not only a leading African-American woman nov-elist, though this is most noteworthy, she is one of the most significant and relevant writers on the literary scene today. Her acclaim is international; her novels are translated into many languages.

Scholars and doctoral candidates the world over critique and assess her works, seeking to unravel the complexity that Morrison prides.[8]

As Ann Geracimos aptly notes, "[Her] life is the stuff of which legends are made, beginning with her childhood growing up poor but proud in the blue-collar town of Lorain, Ohio, where she had a job cleaning houses after school."[9]

Her acclaim should not surprise anyone visiting Morrison's magical world of fiction. After all, in her world anything can, and does, happen.

CHRONOLOGY

1931—Born on February 18 in Lorain, Ohio.

1949—Graduates with honors from Lorain High School.

1949—Attends Howard University in Washington, D.C. Begins to use the name "Toni."

1953—Graduates from Howard University with degree in English.

1955—Graduates from Cornell University in Ithaca, New York, with a master's of arts degree in English.

1955–57—Begins teaching job at Texas Southern University in Houston, Texas.

1957—Begins new teaching position at Howard University in Washington, D.C.

1958—Marries Harold Morrison.

1961—Gives birth to first son, Harold Ford.

1962—Joins a writer's group at Howard University. Writes short story about a girl who wants blue eyes. Later turns it into a novel.

1964—Leaves Howard after marriage ends. Returns home to Lorain, Ohio. Son Slade Kevin born.

1965—Moves to Syracuse, N.Y., for editing job at a division of Random House publishing company.

1967—Moves to New York City to work as senior editor in Random House's company headquarters.

1970—Publishes *The Bluest Eye*.

1971–72—Works as an associate professor at the State University of New York in Purchase, New York.

1973—Publishes *Sula*.

1974—*The Black Book*, edited by Morrison, is published.

1975—*Sula* nominated for National Book Award for fiction. Morrison's father dies in September.

1976–97—Becomes visiting lecturer at Yale University in New Haven, Connecticut.

1977—Publishes *Song of Solomon*. It wins two awards: American Academy and Institute of Arts and Letters Award and the National Book Critics Circle Award. President Carter names her to National Council on the Arts.

1981—*Tar Baby* published.

1983—Morrison ends 20-year career with Random House.

1984—Works as a professor at the State University of New York at Albany.

1986—*Dreaming Emmett* opens in Albany on January 4.

1986–88—Serves as Visiting Lecturer at Bard College in New York.

1987—Publishes *Beloved*.

1988—Receives the Pulitzer Prize in fiction for *Beloved*.

1989–Present—Leads Princeton University's Humanities department. Makes history as first black to hold such a position at an Ivy League college.

1992—Releases *Jazz*.
Publishes *Playing in the Dark: Whiteness and the Literary Imagination*, a book of essays.
Jazz and Playing in the Dark appear on *New York Times* Best-Seller List.
Edits *Race-ing Justice, En-gendering Power: Essays on Anita Hill, Clarence Thomas, and the Construction of Social Reality* (essay collection).

1993—Becomes first black woman to receive the Nobel Prize for Literature.
Swedish Postal Service releases postal stamp.
The Toni Morrison Society established (May).

1994—Mother dies in February.

1995—Attends ribbon-cutting ceremony for the Toni Morrison Reading Room.
Receives Matrix Awards (book category).
Gets honorary Doctor of Humane Letters from Howard University.

1996—Releases *The Dancing Mind* in print and on audiocassette.

1998—Releases *Beloved* the movie.
Publishes *Paradise*.

1999—Publishes *The Big Box*, a children's book co-authored with son Slade.

2000—Releases audiobook of *The Bluest Eye*.

2002—Oprah Winfrey's Book Club features *Sula*.
The Book of Mean People debuts.

2003—Publishes *Love*.
Releases *The Ant or Grasshopper?* and *The Lion or the Mouse?*
Agrees to write *Margaret Garner*.

2004—Publishes *The Poppy or the Snake?* in the *Who's Got Game?* series.
Releases *Remember: The Journey to School Integration*.

2005—*Margaret Garner* opera debuts.
Wins Coretta Scott King Award for *Remember: The Journey to School Integration*.

CHAPTER NOTES

CHAPTER 1. HIP-HOP TALES

1. Toni Morrison and Slade Morrison, *Who's Got Game? The Ant or The Grasshopper?* (New York: Scribner, 2003), p. 1.

2. Ibid., inside front cover flap.

3. Ibid., p. 2.

4. Penguin Group (USA), "The Books of Toni Morrison," *Penguin Putnam Reading Guides,* <http://www.penguinputnam.com/static/rguides/us/toni_morrison.html> (May 14, 2004).

5. *Encyclopedia.com*, "Harlem Renaissance," <http://www.encyclopedia.com/html/h/harlemr1en.asp> (May 16, 2005).

6. Beth Rowen and Borgna Brunner, "Great Days in Harlem: The Birth of the Harlem Renaissance," *Infoplease*, n.d., <http://www.infoplease.com/spot/bhmharlem1.html> (May 16, 2005).

7. *Encyclopedia.com*, "Harlem Renaissance."

8. Ibid.

9. Ibid.

10. Toni Morrison, transcript of January 21, 1998, online chat, <http://www.time.com/time/community/transcripts/chattr012198.html> (February 27, 2005).

11. "The Books of Toni Morrison," <http:// www.penguinputnam.com/static/rguides/us/toni_ morrison.html> (February 27, 2005).

12. Zia Jaffrey, "The Salon interview—Toni Morrison," *Salon*, February 2, 1998, <http://dir. salon.com/books/int/1998/02/02/cov_si_02int/index. html?pn=1> (April 26, 2004).

13. "Toni Morrison's Gift," *Boston Globe*, October 8, 1993, p. 22.

14. Toni Morrison, *Song of Solomon* (New York: Plume, 1987), p. 337.

15. Barbara Hill Rigney, *The Voices of Toni Morrison*, (Columbus, OH: Ohio State University Press, 1991), p. 8.

16. Toni Morrison, *The Bluest Eye* (New York: Plume, 1994), p.58.

17. Barbara Christian, *Black Feminist Criticism* (New York: Teachers College Press, 1991), p. 47.

18. Wilfred D. Samuels and Clenora Hudson-Weems, *Toni Morrison* (Boston: Twayne Publishers, 1990), p. x.

19. Christian, p. 79

20. Kathy Sun, "Morrison Discusses Her Novels and Shares Her Ideas," *Tech 112*, no. 24, May 1, 1992, p. 12, <http://www-tech.mit.edu/V112/N24/morrison. 24a.html> (May 16, 2005).

21. Trudier Harris, "Toni Morrison: Solo Flight through Literature into History," *World Literature Today 68*, no.1, 1994, pp. 9–14, <http://ww.questia.com> (September 20, 2004).

CHAPTER 2. AN AUTHOR'S WORK

1. Denise Heinze, *The Dilemma of "Double-Consciousness"* (Georgia: University of Georgia Press, 1993), p. 3.

2. Penguin Group (USA), "The Books of Toni Morrison," *Penguin Putnam Reading Guides*, <http://www.penguinputnam.com/static/rguides/us/toni_morrison.html> (May 14, 2004).

3. Trudier Harris, "Toni Morrison: Solo Flight Through Literature into History," *World Literature Today,* 68, no. 1, 1994, pp. 9–14, <http://ww.questia.com> (September 20, 2004).

4. Bonnie Angelo, "The Pain of Being Black," *Time*, May 22, 1989, <http://www.time.com/time/community/pulitizerinterview.html> (May 14, 2004).

5. Ibid.

6. Ibid.

7. Penguin Group (USA), "The Books of Toni Morrison."

8. Barbara Hill Rigney, *The Voices of Toni Morrison* (Columbus, OH: Ohio State University Press, 1991), p. 44.

9. 1 Corinthians 3:1–2 (New King James Version).

10. Toni Morrison, *The Bluest Eye* (New York: Plume, 1994) p. 46.

11. "Best 100 Characters in Fiction Since 1900," *Book Magazine*, March-April 2002, p. 38, <http://www.questia.com> (May 10, 2004).

12. Toni Morrison, *Song of Solomon* (New York: Plume, 1994), p. 323.

13. Ibid., p. 128.

14. Toni Morrison, *Beloved* (New York: Plume, 1988), p. 3.

15. Ibid, p. 275.

16. Morrison, *The Bluest Eye*, p. 13.

17. Adam Langer, "*Love* is Toni Morrison's Best Novel in More than a Decade. Now She's Aiming Even Higher," *Book Magazine*, November-December 2003, <http://ww.questia.com> (May 10, 2004).

18. Barbara Christian, *Black Feminist Criticism* (New York: Teachers College Press, 1991), p. 172.

19. Ibid., p. 17.

20. Rigney, p. 36.

21. Marla W. Iyasere and Solomon O. Iyasere, eds., *Understanding Toni Morrison's* Beloved *and* Sula: *Selected Essays and Criticisms of the Works by the Nobel Prize–Winning Author* (Troy, NY: Whitston Publishing, 2000), p. xiv.

22. Karen Carmean, *Toni Morrison's World of Fiction* (Troy, NY: Whitston Publishing, 1993), p. 15.

23. Maria Lauret, contributor, *Liberating Literature: Feminist Fiction in America* (New York: Routledge, 1994), p. 142.

24. Zia Jaffrey, "The *Salon* Interview—Toni Morrison," *Salon*, February 2, 1998, <http://dir.salon.com/books/int/1998/02/02/cov_si_02int/index.html?pn=1> (April 26, 2004).

25. Ibid.

CHAPTER 3. THE DANCING MIND

1. Martha Teichera, "Toni Morrison: Words of Love," *CBS News Sunday Morning*, April 4, 2004, <http://www.cbsnews.com/stories/2004/04/02/sunday/main610053.shtml> (May 15, 2004).

2. Lisa Clayton Robinson, "Toni Morrison," *Encarta Africana*, <http://www.africana.research/encarta/tt_196.asp> (May 16, 2005).

3. Toni Morrison, *Beloved* (New York: Plume, 1988), p. 58.

4. Danuta Bois, "Toni Morrison," *Distinguished Women of Past and Present: Toni Morrison*, 1996, <http:www.distinguishedwomen.com/biographies/morrison.html> (September 18, 2004).

5. Trudier Harris, "Toni Morrison: Solo Flight through Literature into History," *World Literature Today* 68, no. 1, 1994, pp. 9–14, <http://ww.questia.com> (September 20, 2004).

6. Penguin Putnam (USA), "The Books of Toni Morrison," *Penguin Putnam Reading Guides*, <http://www.penguinputnam.com/static/rguides/us/toni_morrison.html> (May 14, 2004).

7. Trudier Harris, "Toni Morrison: Solo Flight through Literature into History."

8. "White House Announces the 2000 National Humanities Medalists," *National Endowment for the Humanities*, December 15, 2000, <http://www.neh.gov/news/archive/20001215.html> (May 16, 2005).

9. Penguin Putnam (USA), "The Books of Toni Morrison."

10. Ann Geracimos, "Writer Toni Morrison through the Eyes of Friends: Always a Champion of Language," *Washington Times*, March 24, 1996, p. 3, <http://www.questia.com> (May, 4, 2004).

11. Elizabeth Farnsworth, "Conversation: Toni Morrison," *The NewsHour with Jim Lehrer Transcript*, March 9, 1998, <http://www.pbs.org/newshour/bb/entertainment/jan-june98/morrison_3-9.html> (April 4, 2004).

12. Ibid.

13. Trudier Harris, "Toni Morrison: Solo Flight through Literature into History."

14. "Faulkner, William," *The Columbia Encyclopedia*, 6th ed., <http://www.questia.com> (May 11, 2004).

15. Barbara Christian, *Black Feminist Criticism* (New York: Teachers College Press, 1991), p. 48.

16. "The South" *The Columbia Encyclopedia*, 6th ed. (New York: Columbia University Press, 2001–04), <http://www.bartleby.com/65/> (April 26, 2004).

17. Trudier Harris, "Toni Morrison: Solo Flight through Literature into History."

CHAPTER 4. IN THE EYE OF THE BEHOLDER

1. Toni Morrison, *The Bluest Eye* (New York: Plume, 1994), p. 174.

2. Karen Carmean, *Toni Morrison's World of Fiction* (Troy, NY: Whitston, 1993), p. 19.

3. Morrison, pp. 210–211.

4. Valerie Boyd, "Black and Blue: An Unforgettable Literary Debut, *The Bluest Eye* Was Toni Morrison's Attempt to Expel the Despair of a Generation," *Book Magazine*, January-February 2003, p. 27, <http://www.questia.com> (May 10, 2004).

5. Ibid.

6. Morrison, p. 209.

7. Barbara Christian, *Black Feminist Criticism* (New York: Teachers College Press, 1991), p. 48.

8. Ibid., p. 48–49.

9. Morrison, p. 118.

10. Cornell West, *Race Matters* (Boston: Beacon Press, 1993), p. 18.

11. Valerie Boyd, "Black and Blue."

12. Ibid.

13. Morrison, p. 210.

14. Ibid., p. 19.

15. Ibid., p. 38.

16. Ibid., p. 39.

17. Ibid., pp. 38–39.

18. Robert Sargent, "A Way of Ordering Experience: A Study of Toni Morrison's *The Bluest Eye* and *Sula*," *Faith of a (Woman) Writer*, eds. Alice Kessler-Harris and William McBrien (New York: Greenwood Press, 1988), p. 231.

19. Ibid., p. 234.

20. Trudier Harris, "Toni Morrison: Solo flight through Literature into History," *World Literature Today* 68, no. 1, 1994, pp. 9–14, <http://www.questia.com> (September 20, 2004).

21. Morrison, p. 45.

22. Ibid., p. 43.

23. Ibid., p. 45.

24. Ibid., p. 117.

25. Barbara Hill Rigney, *The Voices of Toni Morrison* (Columbus, OH: Ohio State University Press, 1991), p. 44.

26. Morrison, p. 182

27. Philip M. Weinstein, *What Else But Love? The Ordeal of Race in Faulkner and Morrison*, (New York: Columbia University Press, 1996), p. 156.

28. Christian, pp. 52–53.

29. Morrison, p. 5.

30. Ibid., p. 17.

31. John Leonard, "Books of the Times," *The New York Times*, November 13, 1970, <http://www.nytimes.com/books/98/01/11/home/morrison-bluest.html> (May 16, 2005).

32. Morrison, p. 216.

33. Adam Langer, "Star Power: *Love* Is Toni Morrison's Best Novel in More than a Decade. Now She's Aiming Even Higher," *Book Magazine*, November-December 2003), p. 40, <http://www.questia.com> (May 10, 2004).

34. Wilfred D. Samuels and Clenora Hudson-Weems, *Toni Morrison* (Boston: Twayne Publishers, 1990), p. 6.

CHAPTER 5. FREEDOM TO FLY

1. Margo Jefferson, "Black Gold," *Newsweek*, September 12, 1997, p. 93.

2. Wilfred D. Samuels and Clenora Hudson-Weems, *Toni Morrison* (Boston: Twayne Publishers, 1990), p. 6.

3. Barbara Christian, *Black Feminist Criticism: Perspectives on Black Women Writers* (New York: Teachers College Press, 1997), p. 61.

4. Toni Morrison, *Song of Solomon* (Plume: New York, 1987), p. 9.

5. Ibid., p. 180.

6. Trudier Harris, "Toni Morrison: Solo Flight through Literature into History," *World Literature Today* 68, no. 1, 1994, pp. 9–14, <http://www.questia.com> (September 30, 2004).

7. Morrison, pp. 10–11.

8. Ibid., p. 11.

9. Robert Sargent, "26 Ways of Ordering Experience: A Study of Toni Morrison's *The Bluest Eye* and *Sula*," *Faith of a Woman Writer*, eds. Alice Kessler-Harris and William McBrien (New York: Greenwood Press, 1988), p. 230.

10. Christian, p. 55.

11. Sargent, p. 231.

12. Trudier Harris, "Toni Morrison: Solo Flight through Literature into History."

13. Patrick Bryce Bjork, *The Novels of Toni Morrison: The Search for Self and Place within the Community* (New York: Peter Lang, 1996), p. 84.

CHAPTER 6. CHASING GHOSTS

1. Trudier Harris, "Toni Morrison: Solo Flight through Literature into History," *World Literature Today* 68, no. 1, 1994, p. 9–14, <http://www.questia.com> (September 30, 2004).

2. "Stampede of Slaves. A Tale of Horror!" *Cincinnati Enquirer*, January 29, 1856, <http://www.enquirer.com/editions/1998/10/02/loc_w_slave02.html> (May 16, 2005).

3. Bonnie Angelo, "The Pain of Being Black," *Time*, May 22, 1989, <http://www.time.com/time/community/pulitzerinterview.html> (May 16, 2005).

4. Toni Morrison, *Beloved* (New York: Plume, 1988), p. 247.

5. Ibid., pp. 198–99.

6. Ibid., p. 219.

7. Ibid., p. 186.

8. Barbara Hill Rigney, *The Voices of Toni Morrison* (Columbus, OH: Ohio State University Press, 1991), p. 41.

9. Peter J. Capuano, "Truth in Timbre: Morrison's Extension of Slave Narrative Song in *Beloved*," *African American Review* 37, no. 1, 2003.

10. Romans 9:25 (New King James Version).

11. Morrison, p. 57.

12. Ibid., p. 66.

13. Ibid., p. 273.

14. Ibid., p. 165.

15. Ibid.

16. Wilfred D. Samuels and Clenora Hudson-Weems, *Toni Morrison* (Boston: Twayne Publishers, 1990), p. 134.

17. Morrison, p. 252.

18. Ibid., pp. 86–87.

19. Ibid., p. 87.

20. Ibid., p. 89.

21. Ibid., p. 184.

22. Rigney, pp. 40–41.

23. Morrison, p. 256.

24. Ibid.

25. Ibid.

26. Ibid.

27. Walter Clemons, "A Gravestone of Memories," *Newsweek*, September 28, 1997, p. 75.

28. Scott Galupo, "Screen Saviors; Good Movies Made from Bad Novels and Vice Versa," *Washington Times*, October 17, 2003, <http://www.questia.com> (May 16, 2005).

29. Adam Langer, "*Love* Is Toni Morrison's Best Novel in More than a Decade. Now She's Aiming Even Higher," *Book Magazine*, November-December 2003, <http://www.questia.com> (May 10, 2004).

CHAPTER 7. SOARING HIGHER

1. John Young, "Toni Morrison, Oprah Winfrey, and Postmodern Popular Audiences," *African American Review*, 35, no. 2, 2001, <http://www.questia.com> (August 5, 2004).

2. Toni Morrison and Slade Morrison, *Who's Got Game? Poppy or The Snake?* (New York: Scribner, 2003), interior cover flap.

3. Dinita Smith, "Toni Morrison's Mix of Tragedy, Domesticity, and Folklore," *The New York Times*, January 8, 1998.

4. Trudier Harris, "Toni Morrison: Solo flight through Literature into History," *World Literature Today,* 68, no. 1, 1994, pp. 9–14, <http://www.questia.com> (September 30, 2004).

5. Ed Bradley, "Justice, Delayed but Not Denied," *CBS News: 60 Minutes,* October 21, 2004 <http://www.cbsnews.com/stories/2004/10/21/60minutes/main650652.shtml>.

6. Joseph C. Phillips, "Standing on Anonymous Shoulders," *Lee Bailey's EURWeb*, <http://www.eurweb.com/story.cfm?id=18577> (May 16, 2005).

7. Ed Bradley, "Justice, Delayed but Not Denied."

8. Wilfred D. Samuels and Clenora Hudson-Weems, *Toni Morrison* (Boston: Twayne Publishers, 1990), p. 142.

9. Ann Geracimos, "Writer Toni Morrison through the Eyes of Friends: Always a Champion of Language," *Washington Times*, March 24, 1966, p. 3, <http://www.questia.com> (May 4, 2004).

GLOSSARY

acquitted—A legal term meaning to be found not guilty in a trial.

adulteress—A single woman who voluntarily has sexual relations with a married man, or a married woman who has sexual relations with someone other than her husband.

alma mater—A school from which a student graduates.

ambiguity—The quality of being obscure, in doubt, or uncertain.

antithesis—The exact opposite.

epitome—The best example of a characteristic of something.

genre—A class of literary works that usually share a common content or style.

irony—A literary device that usually expresses the opposite, rather than the actual or literal meaning, of a word or phrase.

legacy—Something passed down from previous generations having a good or negative influence.

metaphor—A literary device in which one thing is

said to be another. *Example: John was a raging bull in the wrestling match.*

mystic—A person who seeks the truth through magical or spiritual means.

protagonist—A main character of a novel, drama, or other literary work.

pseudonym—A fictitious name by which a writer chooses to be known; a pen name.

reincarnation—A belief that a person's soul can return after death in another form (human, animal, or otherwise).

sermon—A religious message or talk usually presented by a member of the clergy.

stereotype—A standard used to define a thing, idea, image, or opinion, in an oversimplified or prejudicial manner.

symbolism—A literary device that uses a person or thing to represent someone or something else.

thesis—A thorough written analysis of a specific subject that students in graduate school must complete.

Major Works by Toni Morrison

Novels:
The Bluest Eye [1970]
Sula [1973]
Song of Solomon [1977]
Tar Baby [1981]
Beloved [1987]
Jazz [1992]
Paradise [1998]
Love [2003]

Children's Books (*coauthored with son Slade Morrison):
The Big Box [1999]*
The Book of Mean People [2002]
Who's Got Game?: The Ant or the Grasshopper? [2003]*
Who's Got Game?: The Lion or the Mouse? [2003]*
Who's Got Game?: Poppy or the Snake? [2003]*
Remember: The Journey to School Integration [2004]

Other Projects (including works edited):

The Black Book [1974]

Dreaming Emmett (play) [1986]

Playing in the Dark: Whiteness and the Literary Imagination [1992]

Race-ing Justice, En-gendering Power: Essays on Anita Hill, Clarence Thomas, and the Construction of Social Reality [1993]

The Dancing Mind [1996]

FURTHER READING

Bloom, Harold, ed. *Toni Morrison*. Broomall, Pa.: Chelsea House, 2004.

Bloom, Harold, ed. *Toni Morrison's* The Bluest Eye. Broomall, Pa.: Chelsea House, 2002.

Carmean, Karen. *Toni Morrison's World of Fiction*. Troy, NY: Whitston, 1993.

Christian, Barbara. *Black Feminist Criticism: Perspectives on Black Writers*. New York: Teachers College Press, 1997.

Griffin, Farah Jasmine. *Who Set You Flowin'? The African-American Migration Narrative*. New York: Oxford University Press, 1995.

Kramer, Barbara. *Toni Morrison: Nobel Prize-Winning Author*. Berkeley Heights, N.J.: Enslow Publishers, 1996.

INTERNET ADDRESSES

The Toni Morrison Society
http://www2.gsu.edu/~wwwtms/about.html

Nobel Prize.org—Toni Morrison's Acceptance Speech
http://nobelprize.org/literature/laureates/1993

Black American Feminism
http://www.library.ucsb.edu/subjects/
blackfeminism/ah_langlit.html

INDEX